THE INTRODUCTORY CHAPTERS OF YĀQŪT'S MU'JAM AL-BULDĀN

THE INTRODUCTORY CHAPTERS OF YĀQŪT'S MUʿJAM AL-BULDĀN

TRANSLATED AND ANNOTATED

BY

WADIE JWAIDEH

THE GEORGE C. KEISER FOUNDATION
WASHINGTON, D.C.

TUTA SUB AEGIDE PALLAS · EJB

LEIDEN
E. J. BRILL
1959

Printed in the Netherlands by E. J. Brill, Leiden

CONTENTS

ACKNOWLEDGEMENTS

I wish to express my gratitude and indebtedness to the late Mr. George C. Keiser for initiating and sponsoring this translation. It was his deep and continued interest in the project, as President of the Keiser Foundation and Chairman of the Foundation's Translation Committee, that made the completion of this work possible.

I wish also to thank the members of the Translation Committee, Dr. Harold W. Glidden, Prof. Majid Khadduri, and Dr. Robert F. Ogden, for their encouragement and valuable advice throughout the time this work was in progress. I further wish to express my appreciation to Dr. Glidden for reading the final manuscript and making many helpful suggestions, and to Dr. Ogden for making available to me the facilities of the Near East Section of the Library of Congress.

I am also grateful for the kind and encouraging words of a number of distinguished scholars who read the manuscript: Sir Hamilton Gibb, Prof. Harry W. Hazard, Dr. George C. Miles, Prof. V. Minorsky, Prof. Hellmut Ritter, Prof. Franz Rosenthal, the late Prof. George Sarton, and Prof. Georgio Levi della Vida. I am especially indebted to Professors Gibb, Minorsky, and Ritter for many valuable suggestions.

Other persons to whom I owe thanks are Mr. Marschal D. Rothe, Jr., for preparing the maps and diagrams; Mr. William Sands, for useful suggestions regarding publication and for his help in reading the proofs; Col. Willard Webb and Mr. Gordon W. Patterson of the Stack and Reader Division of the Library of Congress, for many kindnesses; the Rev. Patrick W. Skehan of the Catholic University of America, for access to the University's collection of oriental works; Miss Florence Mahorney and Miss Dorothy Paquette, for their assistance in preparing parts of the manuscript; and my wife, who prepared the final copy for the press.

Finally, my sincere thanks are due to Mrs. Nancy Hull Keiser who, after her husband's death, completed the arrangements for the publication of this work.

W. J.

TRANSLATOR'S PREFACE

It is beyond the purpose of this preface to discuss Yāqūt's life or to undertake a detailed evaluation of the *Mu'jam* and its sources. [1] The following observations, which include a brief survey of the literature that has grown around the *Mu'jam* and some of its more recently discovered sources, are merely intended to introduce the present work to the reader.

The important place that this work occupies in medieval Arabic literature has long been recognized both in the east and in the west. J. H. Kramers has described it as "the most complete compilation of the descriptive, astronomical, philological, and traveler's geographical material collected by preceding generations." [2] For more than seven hundred years, the *Mu'jam* has been a rich source of much valuable information on the geography, history and culture of the Muslim world, up to the first quarter of the thirteenth century. The diversified interests of the author, his predilection for detail, and his deliberate striving for erudition in an age when learning was regarded as a form of piety, resulted in a work of vast proportions.

The concept of this enormous compendium was neither Yāqūt's creation nor his peculiar contribution to Arab culture. It rather was a typical product of the times and the intellectual climate in which he lived. For Yāqūt lived at a time when Islamic culture seemed to have exhausted its creative impulse. Men of learning in many parts of the Muslim world were engaged in gathering, organizing, and systematizing the vast body of knowledge left them by the more original and daring minds of the past. Thus encyclopedic compilations such as those of Yāqūt, al-Qalqashandi, and Ibn Faḍl Allāh al-'Umari came to supplant the creative works of al-Bīrūni, Ibn Rushd, and al-Ghazzāli. [3]

Although the *Mu'jam* has been greatly valued throughout the Arab world ever since its appearance, its great size seems to have prompted several abridgements. It was abridged as early as the fourteenth century by Ibn 'Abd al-Ḥaqq in his now famous *Marāṣid al-Iṭṭilā'*. [4] Almost a century later, Jalāl ad-Dīn as-Suyūṭi is reported to have made another abridgement entitled *Mukhtaṣar*

[1] For a brief account of Yāqūt's life and works, see R. Blachère, "Yāḳūt Al-Rūmī," *E.I.*

[2] J. H. Kramers, "Djughrāfiyā," *E. I.*

[3] It may be argued that Islamic civilization was still capable of producing Ibn Khaldūn in the fourteenth century, just as Byzantine civilization had been capable of producing Michael Psellus in the eleventh century. But these were lone figures—the last flicker of a dying fire.

[4] 'Abd al-Mu'min ibn 'Abd al-Ḥaqq, *Marāṣid al-Iṭṭilā' 'ala Asmā' al-Amkinah w-al-Biqā'*, ed. Th. W. Juynboll (Leyden, 1851-64), 6 vols. In his introduction (pp. 1-3), the author points out the excessive length of the *Mu'jam*, stating that he has eliminated all non-geographical material found therein and has revised it wherever necessary, especially with regard to the districts around Baghdad.

Muʿjam al-Buldān. [1] In addition to these two works, Yāqūt himself prepared an abridgement of the *Muʿjam* in which he included similar or identical place names applied to different localities. [2]

The *Muʿjam* has assumed a new importance in modern times. The great need for information of all descriptions on the Islamic countries brought about by the sudden and unprecedented growth of oriental studies in the west at the beginning of the nineteenth century, coupled with the dearth of adequate sources at the time, was bound to produce such a result. The fact that the primary sources utilized by Yāqūt were still largely undiscovered further increased the dependence of scholars upon this work.

No doubt the full significance of Yāqūt's work can be appreciated only when one realizes the extent to which it has been drawn upon by countless writers. For obvious reasons, no attempt will be made here to enumerate all the studies that have utilized the *Muʿjam* as a source of information, despite its fundamental importance in such works as Le Strange's *Lands of the Eastern Caliphate* and Schwarz's *Iran im Mittelalter.* [3] However, a measure of the richness and diversity of the contents of the *Muʿjam,* as well as its importance to nineteenth and twentieth century orientalism, may be gained from the following brief survey of a special category of studies based upon it. All of these studies or portions of them have been based entirely upon individual sections of the *Muʿjam* or upon extracts from it pertaining to specific topics.

The first of these studies in point of time is found in C. M. J. Fraehn, *Ibn-Foszlan's und anderer Araber Berichte über die Russen älterer Zeit und ihre Nachbarn* (St. Petersburg, 1823). [4] This work was based upon extracts from Ibn Faḍlān's *risālah* found in the *Muʿjam,* as well as upon texts from various Arabic sources pertaining to early Russian and Slavic history. This was followed by Kurd de Schloezer, *Abu Dolef Misaris ben Mohalhal de itinere asiatico commentarius* (Berlin, 1845), a study of extracts from Abu Dulaf's *risālahs* as they appear in the *Muʿjam.* A collection of texts from various Arabic sources pertaining to the history, geography and culture of Sicily, including relevant material from Yāqūt, was published by Michele Amari in his *Biblioteca Arabo-Sicula* (Leipzig, 1857). C. Barbier de Meynard's *Dictionnaire Géographique, Historique et Littéraire de la Perse et des Contrées Adjacentes, Extrait du Modjem El-Bouldan de Yaqout* (Paris, 1861), the best work on the geography of Persia in the nineteenth century, was based almost entirely upon the *Muʿjam.*

Texts relating to pre-Islamic Arab paganism were studied by Ludolf Krehl

[1] Ḥājji Khalīfah, probably the first writer to have mentioned the abridgements of Ibn ʿAbd al-Ḥaqq and as-Suyūṭi, seems to have confounded the two works. For he quotes most of Ibn ʿAbd al-Ḥaqq's introduction, attributing it to as-Suyūṭi. On the confusion regarding this matter, see Ḥājji Khalīfah, *Kashf aẓ-Ẓunūn,* II, 1733-34; J. T. Reinaud, *Géographie d'Aboulféda: I. Introduction Générale,* pp. cxxxiv-cxxxv; and Wüstenfeld, *Die Geschichtschreiber der Araber und ihre Werke* (Göttingen, 1882), No. 506, p. 232. According to *G.A.L. Supp.* I, 880, a copy of as-Suyūṭi's *Mukhtaṣar* is found in the Āṣafīyah collection in Ḥaydarābād.

[2] Yāqūt, *Al-Mushtarik Waḍʿan w-al-Mukhtalif Ṣaqʿan,* ed. Wüstenfeld (Göttingen, 1846).

[3] It is interesting to note that the *Muʿjam* has been drawn upon not only by Arab lexicographers such as az-Zabīdi, but also by Western lexicographers such as Dozy, Lane, and Fleischer. See Reinaud, "Notice sur les Dictionnaires Géographiques Arabes," *J.A.* (Août-Sept. 1860), XVI, 65-106.

[4] Fraehn's study inaugurated an enormous amount of literature on the Arabic sources of early Russian and Slavic history. For a bibliography, see V. Minorsky, *Ḥudūd,* pp. 425-427.

in his *Über die Religion der Vorislamischen Araber* (Leipzig, 1863). These texts, which consisted of extracts from Ibn al-Kalbi's *Kitāb al-Aṣnām* as found in Yāqūt, were made available to the author by Wüstenfeld while the latter was still engaged in editing the *Mu'jam*. More than thirty years later, J. Wellhausen, in his *Reste arabischen Heidentums* (Berlin, 1897), translated and annotated all the extracts in Yāqūt from Ibn al-Kalbi's book (pp. 10-64). A study of the *ḥarrah*-lands of Arabia by Otto Loth, based upon all the entries on this topic in the *Mu'jam*, appeared under the title "Die Vulkanregionen (Ḥarra's) von Arabien nach Jaḳut," in *ZDMG* (1868), XXII, 365-382. Various extracts from the *Mu'jam* pertaining to the Crusades provided the basis for Hartwig Derenbourg's study, "Les Croisades d'après le dictionnaire de Yakout," *Centenaire de l'Ecole des Langues Orientales Vivantes* 1795-1895 (Paris, 1895), pp. 71-92. Ernst Dammann's *Beiträge aus arabischen Quellen zur Kenntnis des negrischen Afrika* (Kiel, 1929), a study of Arabic sources pertaining to Negro Africa, was based almost entirely upon entries found in the *Mu'jam* and in al-Qazwīni's *Kosmographie*.

An event of great importance for all students of Muslim culture was the publication in 1866 of Wüstenfeld's edition of the *Mu'jam*. [1] Besides editing this work and making it available to the general public, Wüstenfeld rendered a further contribution by providing valuable notes and indices which laid the foundation for a systematic study of the *Mu'jam* and its sources. [2] While engaged in editing the dictionary, Wüstenfeld published two articles on Yāqūt's travels and their relation to the *Mu'jam*. [3]

In 1898 Heer published what is still the best and most comprehensive study of the *Mu'jam* and its sources. [4] Interest in Yāqūt has been kept alive since then by the discovery and publication of a number of his sources. Aḥmad Zaki Pasha in 1914 published Ibn al-Kalbi's *Kitāb al-Aṣnām*, or *Kitāb Tankīs al-Aṣnām*, from a rare manuscript in his possession. [5] This resulted in a number of studies which added much to the earlier studies of Krehl and Wellhausen based on extracts from Yāqūt's texts. [6]

The discovery in 1923 by A. Z. Validi Togan of the Mashhad Ms. containing the second half of Ibn al-Faqīh's work, the two *risālahs* of Abu Dulaf Mis'ar

[1] *Jacut's geographisches Wörterbuch*, ed. F. Wüstenfeld (Leipzig, 1866-72), 6 vols.

[2] The usefulness of the *Mu'jam* has been further enhanced by Rescher's index to Wüstenfeld's edition, published more than half a century later. See Oskar Rescher, *Sachindex zu Wüstenfeld's Ausgabe von Jaqut's "Mu'ǧam al-Buldān"* (Stuttgart, 1928).

[3] F. Wüstenfeld, "Jâcût's Reisen, aus seinem geographischen Wörterbuche beschrieben," *ZDMG* (1864) XVIII, 397-493, and "Der Reisende Jâcût als Schriftsteller und Gelehrter," *Nachrichten von der Königl. Gesellschaft der Wissenschaften* (Göttingen, 1865) No. 9, pp. 233-243.

[4] F. Justus Heer, *Die historischen und geographischen Quellen in Jacut's geographischem Wörterbuch* (Strassburg, 1898).

[5] A second edition of this work was published by Aḥmad Zaki Pasha in 1924.

[6] In 1926 M. S. Marmardji published a French translation of most of the material found in the 1914 edition of *Kitāb al-Aṣnām*. See M. S. Marmardji, "Les Dieux de Paganisme Arabe, d'après Ibn al-Kalbi," *Revue Biblique* (Paris, 1926) XXXV, 397-420. For a German translation and commentary, see Rosa Klinke-Rosenberger, *Das Götzenbuch Kitâb al-Aṣnâm* (Zürich, 1942). For an English translation with an introduction and notes, see Nabih Amin Faris, *The Book of Idols* (Princeton, 1952).

ibn al-Muhalhil [1], and the *risālah* of Ibn Faḍlān [2] has stimulated an already impressive mass of literature with much bearing on Yāqūt. Another source of the *Muʿjam*, ash-Shābushti's *Kitāb ad-Diyārāt*—one of the most celebrated works on Christian monasteries in the Muslim world—was recently published for the first time in Baghdad. [3]

No doubt further research will continue to add to our already extensive knowledge of Yāqūt and his sources. In a recent issue of the Iraqi Academy's Journal, Shaykh Muḥammad Riḍā' ash-Shabībi has referred to Yāqūt's unacknowledged borrowings from a number of authors, particularly al-Qāḍi ʿAyāḍ, and promised to deal with the matter in a more detailed study. [4]

It may be appropriate at this point to say a few words about Yāqūt and his work. Far from being an indiscriminate compiler, he often has proved himself to be a writer of considerable critical acumen. His spirited defense of Ibn al-Kalbi, despite the fact that the latter's unorthodox methods of investigation were suspect to many leading scholars at the time, does credit to his sound sense of judgment. [5] His admiration for al-Bīrūni, upon whom he draws so extensively

[1] See A. von Rohr-Sauer, *Des Abū Dulaf Bericht über seine Reise nach Turkestan, China und Indien* (Bonn, 1939). This is a study of Abu Dulaf's first *risālah* with a translation and commentary. For an evaluation of this study, see Hans von Mžik's critical review in *OLZ* (1942) No. 5, pp. 240-242. On Abu Dulaf's second *risālah*, see V. Minorsky, "La deuxième risala d'Abu-Dulaf," *Oriens* (1952) V, No. 1, pp. 23-27. In addition to dealing with the second *risālah*, this article discusses the first *risālah* as well as Von Rohr-Sauer's study. For a brief account of Abu Dulaf's life and his reliability as an author, see V. Minorsky, "Abu Dulaf," *E.I.* (new edition). Professor Minorsky informed me in December 1955 that he had just received the first copy of his book *Abu Dulaf Misʿar ibn al-Muhalhil's Travels in Iran* (Cairo, 1955).

[2] See: (a) A. P. Kovalevskii, "Novootkrytyi tekst Ibn-Fadlana," *Vestnik drevnei istorii* (Moscow, 1938) 1 (2), pp. 57-71, an article dealing with the newly discovered Ms. and the Russian edition then being prepared under the direction of Krachkovskii; the writer discusses the content and gives a brief synopsis of the use made by Yāqūt of Ibn Faḍlān's material.

(b) *Puteshestvie Ibn-Fadlana na Volgu*, perevod i kommentarii pod redaktsiei akademika I. Y. Krachkovskogo, Izdatel'stvo Akademii Nauk SSSR (Moscow, Leningrad, 1939), photographed Arabic text with Russian translation and commentary prepared under the direction of I. Y. Krachkovskii. (c) A. Zeki Validi Togan, *Ibn Fadlan's Reisebericht*, Abhandlungen für die Kunde des Morgenlandes (Leipzig, 1939), Bd. XXIV, 3, German translation and commentary with printed Arabic text. (d) Hellmut Ritter, "Zum Text von Ibn Fadlan's Reisebericht," *ZDMG* (1942) XCVI, I, 98-126, a review of A.Z.V. Togan's edition with critical notes. (e) R. P. Blake and R. N. Frye, "Notes on the Risala of Ibn Fadlan," *Byzantina-Metabyzantina* (1949) I, 7-37, English version with notes. (f) D. M. Dunlop, "Zeki Validi's Ibn Fadlān," *Die Welt des Orients* (Stuttgart, 1949), pp. 307-316, a review of A.Z.V. Togan's edition with a critical discussion of Yāqūt's use of Ibn Faḍlān's material. (g) A. P. Kovalevskii, "O stepeni dostovernosti Ibn-Fadlana," *Istoricheskie Zapiski* (1950) XXXV, 265-293, a discussion of the reliability of Ibn Faḍlan, shedding considerable light on Yāqūt's attitude toward Ibn Faḍlān as a source. (h) K. Czeglédy, "Zur Meschheder Handschrift von Ibn Fadlan's Reisebericht," *Acta Orientalia*, Academiae Scientiarum Hungaricae (Budapest, 1951) I, Fasc. 2-5, pp. 218-260, a critical review of the various texts and editions of Ibn Faḍlān's *risālah*, together with photographic reproductions of the Arabic text.

[3] Ash-Shābushti, *Kitāb ad-Diyārāt*, edited with annotations by Gurgīs ʿAwwād (Baghdad, 1951). The numerous passages extracted by Yāqūt from ash-Shābushti receive much attention from the editor. Corresponding passages from the two works are collated, with valuable results for both texts, and a number of extracts from Yāqūt are used by the editor to provide information on several monasteries that is missing from the partly damaged Berlin Ms. upon which this edition is based. For a review of this work, see H. Ritter, *Oriens* (1952), V, no. 2, pp. 366-368.

[4] Muḥammad Riḍā' ash-Shabībi, "Aqdam Makhṭūṭ Waṣala Ilayna min Bilād al-ʿArab," *Majallat al-Majmaʿ al-ʿIlmi al-ʿIrāqi* (Baghdad, 1950) I, p. 40.

[5] For Yāqūt on Ibn al-Kalbi, see *Muʿjam* II, 158, 652. Referring to Hishām ibn al-Kalbi and his father, Brockelmann says, "Modern research has confirmed many of their statements,

in the introductory chapters, is another indication of his judiciousness as a compiler. [1] However, it should be pointed out here that Yāqūt, as Professor Minorsky has indicated, displays at times a certain degree of arbitrariness in the treatment of his sources. [2] Perhaps the alphabetical arrangement of the *Muʿjam* is partly responsible for this. For in a work of this nature it is not easy for the compiler to preserve the unity of the original source when selecting data appropriate for inclusion under the various entries.

The introductory chapters are perhaps the least known and the most neglected part of the *Muʿjam*. Various writers have dealt with isolated parts of these chapters—as will be seen from the annotations that accompany this translation—and others such as Reinaud, Barbier de Meynard, and Blachère have made a synopsis of their contents. [3] However, no attempt has so far been made to undertake a systematic and critical study of this portion of the *Muʿjam*.

Despite this strange neglect of the introductory chapters, there can be no doubt of their importance. For in them Yāqūt not only explains the scope and method of his entire work, but also presents cosmological and geographical ideas prevalent in his day, defines various geographical terms, discusses legal concepts pertaining to conquered lands under Muslim law, and gives a few samples of stories on the qualities of peoples and countries representative of a certain genre of literature then popular in the Islamic world.

This translation has been based upon the two [4] existing editions of the *Muʿjam*: Ferdinand Wüstenfeld's *Jacut's geographisches Wörterbuch* (Leipzig, 1866-71), 6 vols.; [5] and Amīn Khānaji's *Kitāb Muʿjam al-Buldān*, (Cairo, 1906-7), 10 vols., including a modern supplement on America, Europe and other regions. These are referred to as the German and the Egyptian editions, respectively. [6] Unless

which they reached sometimes by regular scientific methods such as the study of inscriptions." C. Brockelmann, "Al-Kalbi," *E.I.* N. A. Faris discusses Ibn al-Kalbi's critics and his defense by al-Masʿūdi and Yāqūt, with an English rendition of the latter's defense. See *The Book of Idols*, (ed. and tr. N. A. Faris), ix.

[1] Referring to the use made by Yāqūt of geographical material in the introductory chapters, Kramers has said that he "deserves much credit for quoting al-Bīrūni so largely in his preface." See J. H. Kramers, "Djughrāfiyā", *E. I.*

[2] V. Minorsky, "La deuxième *Risāla*," *Oriens* (1952) V, No. 1, p. 23.

[3] J. T. Reinaud, *Géographie d'Aboulféda* (Paris, 1848), I, cxxxi-cxxxii, and his "Notice sur les Dictionnaires Géographiques Arabes," *J.A.* (Août-Sept. 1860) XVI, 85-86; Barbier de Meynard, *Dictionnaire de la Perse*, pp. vii-xiv; and R. Blachère, *Extraits des Principaux Géographes Arabes du Moyen Age* (Paris, Beirut, 1932), pp. 265-266.

[4] Reference should be made here to the latest edition of the *Muʿjam* published by the Ṣādir company of Beirut, Lebanon. This work, which began to appear in fascicule form in 1955, was completed in twenty fascicules in 1957. It should be pointed out that this is not a critical edition and does not supersede either of the two earlier editions upon which it has obviously been based. Corrupt passages, misspelled proper names, incorrect figures and other errors found in the German and the Egyptian editions stand uncorrected. While a number of grammatical and typographical errors have been corrected, the new edition lacks the valuable indices of the German edition. Nevertheless, its publication is both timely and welcome, since the previous editions are out of print and difficult to obtain. It should be noted that this translation was completed in the autumn of 1954, almost a year before the Ṣādir edition began to appear. For this reason, the new edition of the *Muʿjam* has not been utilized in this work.

[5] An anastatic reprint of this edition appeared in 1924.

[6] Although only one Egyptian edition of the *Muʿjam* is known to exist, there are a number of unaccountable discrepancies between the two copies in the possession of the Library of Congress. The last line of the title page of one copy reads as follows: "Ṭubiʿa bi-maṭbaʿat as-Saʿādah bi-jiwār Muḥāfaẓat Miṣr." The other has the additional information "li-Ṣāḥibiha Muḥammad Ismāʿīl." In order to distinguish between the two copies in certain cases where discrepancies occur, the former will be referred to as the Egyptian edition, the latter as the Egyptian edition (M.I.). Otherwise reference will be made only to the Egyptian edition.

otherwise specified, all footnote references to the *Muʿjam* are to the German edition.

In the text of this translation, parentheses have been used to enclose English equivalents of Arabic terms and place names or vice versa, while square brackets have been used to enclose words or phrases supplied by the translator for purposes of clarity.

The annotations are designed to shed as much light on the text as possible. With this object in mind, technical terms have been explained and appropriate references given, parallel texts have been cited, and brief biographical notes pertaining to persons mentioned in the text have been provided. Unacknowledged borrowings, statements of undetermined origin (e.g., those on the nature of the universe attributed to "the ancients"), and those passages not identified beyond the mere mention of the author's name, have been traced to their original sources and exact references given. Obscure or mutilated passages resulting from a corrupt text, erroneous figures and measurements, misspelled place names and other textual errors have been corrected whenever possible. Collation has not been limited to the German and Egyptian editions of the *Muʿjam*; other sources have also been used for purposes of comparison.

The system of transliteration used by the U. S. Board on Geographical Names has been followed with slight modifications. Forms of certain place names long prevalent in English, such as Mecca, Aden, etc., have been adopted. Pious formulas following the name of God, the Prophet, and the Companions have been eliminated in order to avoid needless repetition. The numbering of Qur'ānic verses in the footnotes follows Flügel's edition of the Qur'ān.

In translating this work, every effort has been made to follow the Arabic text as closely as possible and to preserve the peculiar style of the author, which for all its ornateness is not without a certain archaic charm.

Washington, D. C., 1956. WADIE JWAIDEH

LIST OF ABBREVIATIONS OF WORKS MOST FREQUENTLY CITED

A.J.S.L.	*American Journal of Semitic Languages and Literatures*
B.G.A.	*Bibliotheca geographorum arabicorum*
al-Bīrūni, *Tafhīm*	*Kitāb at-Tafhīm li-Awā'il Ṣinā'at at-Tanjīm*, ed. R. Ramsey Wright (London, 1934)
Burnet, *E.G.P.*	*Early Greek Philosophy* (London, 1920)
C.T.M.	Wensinck, et al, *Concordance et indices de la tradition musulmans* (Leyden, 1933-)
Diels, *Vors.*	*Die Fragmente der Vorsokratiker, griechisch und deutsch.* 6 verb. Aufl. Hrsg. von Walter Kranz (Berlin, 1951-52), 3 vols.
E.I.	*The Encyclopaedia of Islam* (Leyden, 1913-36)
E.I. Supp.	*The Encyclopaedia of Islam Supplement* (Leyden, 1939)
E.I. (New ed.)	*The Encyclopaedia of Islam*, New edition (Leyden, 1954-)
Ferrand, *Relations de voyages*	*Relations de voyages et textes geographiques Arabes, Persans et Turks relatifs a l'Extreme-Orient du VIIIe au XVIIIe siecles* (Paris, 1913-14), 2 vols.
Freeman, *Ancilla*	*Ancilla to the Pre-Socratic Philosophers* (Oxford, 1944)
Freeman, *Companion*	*Companion to the Pre-Socratic Philosophers* (Oxford, 1949)
G.A.L.	Brockelmann, *Geschichte der arabischen Litteratur* (Leyden, 1943-49), 2 vols.
G.A.L. Supp.	Brockelmann, *Geschichte der arabischen Litteratur Supplementband* (Leyden, 1937-42), 3 vols.
Ḥājji Khalīfa, *Kashf aẓ-Ẓunūn*	*Kitāb Kashf aẓ-Ẓunūn 'an Asāmi al-Kutub w-al-Funūn*, ed. S. Yaltakya and Kilisli Rifat Bilge (Istanbul, 1941-43), 2 vols.
Ibn al-Faqīh, *B.G.A.*, V	*Mukhtaṣar Kitāb al-Buldān*, ed. M. J. de Goeje (Leyden, 1885)
Ibn Ḥawqal, *B.G.A.*, II	*Kitāb Ṣūrat al-Arḍ*, ed. J. H. Kramers (Leyden, 1938-39)
Ibn Khurradādhbih, *B.G.A.*, VI	*al-Masālik w-al-Mamālik*, ed. M. J. de Goeje (Leyden, 1889)
Ibn an-Nadīm, *al-Fihrist*	*Kitāb al-Fihrist*, ed. G. Flügel (Leipzig, 1871-72).
Ibn Rustah, *B.G.A.*, VII	*Kitāb al-A'lāq an-Nafīsa*, ed. M. J. de Goeje (Leyden,1892)
Ibn Sa'd, *Kitāb aṭ-Ṭabaqāt*	*Kitāb aṭ-Ṭabaqāt al-Kabīr*, ed. E. Sachau et al (Leyden, 1905-40)
al-Iṣṭakhri, *B.G.A.*, I	*al-Masālik w-al-Mamālik*, ed. M. J. de Goeje (Leyden 1927)
al-Khwarizmi, *Mafātīḥ al-'Ulūm*	*Kitāb Mafātīḥ al-'Ulūm*, ed. G. van Vloten (Leyden, 1895)
Lane, *Lexicon*	*An Arabic-English Lexicon* (London, 1863-93)
al-Maqdisi, *B.G.A.*, III	*Aḥsan at-Taqāsīm fi Ma'rifat al-Aqālīm*, ed. M. J. de Goeje (Leyden, 1906)
al-Mas'ūdi, *B.G.A.*, VIII	*Kitāb at-Tanbīh w-al-Ishrāf*, ed. M. J. de Goeje (Leyden, 1894)
al-Mas'ūdi, *Murūj*	*Murūj adh-Dhahab*, ed. Barbier de Meynard and Pavet de Courteille (Paris, 1861-77), 9 vols.
Minorsky, *Ḥudūd*	*Ḥudūd al-'Ālam*, trans. and ed. V. Minorsky, GMS, N.S. XI (London, 1937)
Minorsky, *Marvazi*	*Sharaf al-Zamān Ṭāhir Marvazi on China, the Turks and India*, trans. and ed. V. Minorsky (London, 1942)
Nallino, *Raccolta*, V	*Raccolta di Scritti editi e inediti* (Rome, 1944), V
an-Nawawi, *Tahdhīb al-Asmā'*	*Tahdhīb al-Asmā' w-al-Lughāt*, ed. F. Wüstenfeld (Göttingen, 1842-47)

O.L.Z.	*Orientalistische Literaturzeitung*
Pauly-Wissowa, *Real-Encyclopädie*	*Real-Encyclopädie der Classischen Altertumswissenschaft*
al-Qazwīni, *ʿAjāʾib*	*ʿAjāʾib al-Makhlūqāt w-Gharāʾib al-Mawjūdāt,* ed. F. Wüstenfeld (Göttingen, 1848-49)
al-Qazwīni, *Āthār al-Bilād*	*Kitāb Āthār al-Bilād w-Akhbār al-ʿIbād,* ed. F. Wüstenfeld (Göttingen, 1847)
S.E.I.	*Shorter Encyclopaedia of Islam* (Leyden, 1953)
Wüstenfeld, *Geschichtschreiber*	*Die Geschichtschreiber der Araber und ihre Werke* (Göttingen, 1882)
Yāqūt, *Irshād*	*Irshād al-Arīb ila Maʿrifat al-Adīb,* ed. D. S. Margoliouth, GMS VI (Leyden, 1907-31)
Z.D.M.G.	*Zeitschrift des Deutschen Morgenlandischen Gesellschaft*

INTRODUCTION

IN THE NAME OF GOD, THE COMPASSIONATE, THE MERCIFUL

PRAISE BE to God who has made the earth like unto an expanse and the mountains like unto stakes, and spread therefrom peaks and gorges, deserts and towns; who has caused rivers to gush forth through the land, and streams and seas to flow; and who has guided His creatures to take dwellings unto themselves and to construct well-made buildings and homes. Whereupon they have raised edifices and founded cities, carved habitations out of mountains, and contrived wells and cisterns. He has made their eagerness to raise that which they have raised and to build that which they have built, a warning to the heedless and an example to following generations. He said, and He is the most truthful of sayers:

> Have they not journeyed through the land and beheld the end of those before them who were more numerous than they and mightier in strength, and who left a greater mark upon the earth? Yet all that of which they possessed themselves availed them not. [1]

I give praise unto Him for that which He has given and bestowed, for inspiring rectitude and guiding to it, for imparting understanding and making wisdom manifest. May God bless Muḥammad—the elect among His prophets and apostles, the most favored among the pious and those beloved of Him, he who was sent with guidance and with the perspicuous religion, of whom it is written, "We sent thee not, save as a mercy to all creatures," [2]—and the noble and saintly members of his household and the select and righteous Companions. May God save and preserve them all.

This is a book on the names of countries; on mountains, valleys, and plains; on villages, post-houses, and dwellings; on seas, rivers, and lakes; on idols, graven images, and objects of heathen worship. I have not undertaken to write this book, nor dedicated myself to composing it, in a spirit of frolic or diversion. Nor have I been impelled to do so by dread or desire; nor moved by longing for my native land; nor prompted by yearning for one who is loving and compassionate. Rather, I considered it my duty to address myself to this task, and, being capable of performing it, I regarded responding to its challenge as an inescapable obligation.

I was made aware of it by the great and glorious Book, and was guided to it by the Great Tidings, wherein God said, glory and majesty to Him, when He wanted to manifest to His creatures His signs and warnings and establish their guilt by visiting upon them His painful wrath:

> Have they not journeyed through the land? And have they not hearts to

[1] Qur'ān XL, 82.
[2] Qur'ān XXI, 107.

understand with, or ears to hear with? Surely as to these things their eyes are not blind, but the hearts which are within their breasts are blind. [1]

This is a reproof to him who has journeyed through the world and has not heeded the warning, and to him who has contemplated the departed centuries and has not been deterred.

God said, and He is the most truthful of sayers:

> Say: Journey through the land and behold the manner in which the disbelievers have met their end. [2]

In other words, consider how their dwelling places were razed, all traces of them obliterated, and their lights extinguished in punishment for disregarding His commandments and transgressing against His prohibitions. This message is found in other unabrogated verses setting forth irrevocable commandments and prohibitions.

The first verse is a reprimand, clearly set forth, because of previous prohibition of the offense. The second is a commandment manifestly prescribing an obligation. This is from the Book of God, which "shall remain untouched by falsehood, in the future as in the past," [3] and which shall never suffer impairment as to its composition or form.

In traditions (*athar*) [4] concerning righteous men of the past, ʿĪsa ibn Maryam (Jesus Son of Mary) is quoted as saying:

> The world is a place of visitation and an abode of transition. Be you then travelers in it, and take warning from what remains of the traces of the early ones.[5]

Quss ibn Sāʿidah, [6] whom the Prophet declared would be resurrected as an *ummah* [7] by himself, said:

[1] Qur'ān XXII, 45.

[2] Qur'ān VI, 11.

[3] Qur'ān XLI, 42.

[4] Here Yāqūt uses the term *athar* in the same sense in which the jurists apply it to the *salaf* (righteous Muslim predecessors whose example is followed in religious and other matters). See Mawlawi Muḥammad Aʿla ibn ʿAli, *The Dictionary of Technical Terms*, ed. Aloys Sprenger and W. Nassau Lees, (Calcutta, 1862), I, 65.

[5] D. S. Margoliouth lists this saying in his "Christ in Islam," *Expository Times*, V (1893-94), 59, but does not trace it beyond Yāqūt. Asín, who has made the fullest study and assembled the largest catena of the words and deeds of Christ in Muslim literature, seems to have overlooked this one. According to the criteria established by him, however, this passage may properly be described as *agrapha*. See Michaël Asín et Palacios, "Logia et Agrapha Domini Jesu," *Patrologia Orientalis*, Vols. XIII and XIX.

[6] Pre-Islamic Christian figure, esteemed for his eloquence and piety. The Prophet is supposed to have had great admiration for Quss. Several accounts tell of the Prophet reminiscing about a sermon of Quss which seems to have made a lasting impression upon him. See article "Ḳuss ibn Sāʿida" by H. Lammens in *E.I.* Other sources on Quss not listed in the above article are: Abu al-Faraj al-Iṣbahāni, *al-Aghāni*, (Cairo, A.H. 1285), XIV, 41-42; al-Masʿūdi, *Murūj adh-Dhahab*, ed. Barbier de Meynard and Pavet de Courteille, (Paris, 1861), I, 357; Abu Ḥātim as-Sijistāni, *Kitāb al-Muʿammarīn*, ed. Ignaz Goldziher, (Leyden, 1899), pp. 76-78; Ibn al-Faqīh, *B.G.A.*, V, 49; and Ibrāhīm ibn Muḥammad al-Bayhaqi, *Kitāb al-Maḥāsin w-al-Masāwi*, ed. Friedrich Schwally, (Leipzig, 1900), pp. 351-354.

[7] This is a rare usage of the word *ummah*. It probably is not duplicated in the whole range of *ḥadīth*. Commenting on this tradition, the authenticity of which he does not seem to doubt, al-Jāḥiẓ refers to the unique honor that it sheds upon Quss and his tribe, an honor not shared by any other man or people. See al-Jāḥiẓ, *al-Bayān w-at-Tabyīn*, (Cairo, A.H. 1311), I, 120. In the Qur'ān there is only one instance of such usage, where this term is applied to Abraham (Qur'ān XVI, 121). Interpreters of the Qur'ān have taken it to mean

The most eloquent of sermons is journeying through the wilderness and contemplating the resting places of the dead. [1]

Poets have praised caliphs, kings, and princes for journeying through the land and for braving high peaks and precipitous gorges. One of them has said in praise of al-Muʿtaṣim: [2]

You ranged with power through all the land,
As though you sought al-Khiḍr's trail. [3]

The means for seeing [various places] may prove impossible of attainment, whereupon it becomes necessary to seek information pertaining thereto. It is therefore incumbent upon us to inform the Muslims of that which we know, and to come to their aid with that which God, in His beneficence, has bestowed upon us. Though the need for this particular knowledge is shared by everyone who has had a measure of learning, has acquired a part or parcel thereof, or who is known by it and bears the impress or the traces of one of its branches, yet I have not come upon anyone who has emended the faulty nomenclature [of geography] or who has felt himself equal to the task of rectifying information concerning the routes and regions pertaining to it. Rather I have found that the majority of the transmitters of the *akhbār* [4] (usages of the Prophet) and the eminent narrators of poetry and the *āthār* [4] (usages of the Companions), who have devoted all their time to these studies and exhausted their lives and efforts in such endeavors, have persevered with success in doing what is right; entering the gardens of wisdom through the gateways of every pursuit, excelling in the

imām (leader or model). See interpretation of surah XVI, verse 121, in *al-Qur'ān al-Karīm: Tafsīr al-Jalālayn*, (Cairo, A.H. 1353), p. 218. See also ʿAbd ar-Ra'ūf al-Miṣri, *Mu'jam al-Qur'ān*, (Jerusalem, 1945), I, 91-93. Translators of the Qur'ān are not agreed on the best rendition of this term into English. Rodwell translates the verse as "Verily, Abraham was a leader in religion," but points out that it may be rendered as "Abraham was a people." Marmaduke Pickthall renders it as "Abraham was a nation." A. Yūsuf 'Ali translates the verse as "Abraham was indeed a model," but adds by way of explanation in a footnote that ". . . the idea that he was an *ummah* in himself standing against his world shall not be lost sight of." For a comprehensive discussion of this term, see article "Umma" by R. Paret in *E.I.* Jalāl ad-Dīn as-Suyūṭi examines this *ḥadīth* critically and concludes that it is not a genuine one. See his *al-La'āli' al-Maṣnūʿah fi al-Aḥādīth al-Mawḍūʿah*. (Cairo, A.H. 1352), 183-192.

[1] This occurs as part of a more detailed statement attributed to Quss ibn Sāʿidah in Ibn al-Faqīh, *B.G.A.*, V, 46, and in al-Bayhaqi, *Kitāb al-Maḥāsin*, p. 353.

[2] The eighth Abbasid caliph. Born *ca.* A.H. 180/A.D. 796-7; died A.H. 227/A.D. 842. See article "Al-Muʿtaṣim" by K.V. Zetterstéen in *E.I.*

[3] Legendary Muslim figure, identified with various prophets and saints such as Enoch, Elijah, and St. George. See article "al-Khiḍr" by A. J. Wensinck in *E.I.* See also Meijer De Hond, *Der Korānisirte Elḥidr*, (Leyden, 1914). The above verse is found in Ibn al-Faqīh, *B.G.A.*, V, 52. It seems that Yāqūt borrowed the idea of extolling the advantages of travel from this writer, who devotes a whole section to traveling in foreign lands.

[4] It should be pointed out here that the definition of *akhbār* (sing. *khabar*) as the usage of the Prophet, and *āthār* (sing. *athar*) as the usage of the Companions, besides being in keeping with the spirit of the text, is the most widely accepted definition. According to Wensinck, al-Ghazzāli applies the term *akhbār* to traditions which go back to Muḥammad, while he distinguishes the sayings of the Companions by the term *āthār*. (See article "Khabar" by A. J. Wensinck in *E.I.*). There seems to be a lack of agreement among Muslim writers, however, regarding the precise meaning and application of these two terms. For the various ways in which they are used by traditionists, jurists and others, see *The Dictionary of Technical Terms*, I, 65, 281, and 410. See also Thomas Patrick Hughes, *A Dictionary of Islam*, (London, 1935), p. 23; Lane's *Lexicon*, under "*athar*" and "*khabar*"; and article "Athar" by I. Goldziher in *E.I.*

various fields of the letters and the sciences; in the recitation of the *sunan* [1] (practices of the Prophet) and the *āthār,* and in the narration of the *ḥadīth* [2] (traditions of the Prophet) and the *akhbār*. For they attain to a knowledge of the meaning of these studies, whereby they deduce the significance of preceding words from those which follow. For words, as it were, are like links in a chain, the end leading to the beginning and the beginning leading to the end.

But when they come upon the name of a place wherein a great battle was fought, they are confounded. For the writer in this case is in need of traditional knowledge (*naql*) rather than reason (*ʿaql*), transmission rather than perception. Consequently, you will find him either erring or prevaricating; he will lower his voice after having raised it, and temper the sharpness of his tongue by restraining it. [3]

I have seldom come upon books, even those written in a fine hand and carefully provided with dots and vowel signs, wherein place names have not been left undotted or altered and thus made to depart from the right path or to deviate from it, the writer in ignorance having left them undotted or having copied them down in error.

How many a venerable *imām,* distinguished nobleman, great prince, or minister of consequence, has been attributed to an unknown place! Upon interpreting conjectures, you will find this place subject to all kinds of speculations. If men of learning are questioned about it, they take refuge in the wretched half of learning, which is, "I know not." Thus the purpose of the honest man is defeated. For if he seeks to establish where the place is, he finds himself in difficulty. His quest, should he pursue one, remains unattained, his efforts ending in perplexity. This situation arises from the neglect of this important branch of knowledge by men of learning, despite its importance, and from their indifference to this great pursuit, despite its grandeur. For what man of perception can afford to dispense with a knowledge of the correct form of place names and the determination of their locations?

The fact that all men alike stand in need of this knowledge accounts for its being a favorite topic of conversation at gatherings. For some of these places are the *mawāqīt* [4] of pilgrims and visitors, the domiciles of the Companions and Followers, the tomb-shrines of the saints and the pious, the scenes of the expeditions of the Master of Apostles [Muḥammad], and the territories conquered by the *imāms,* the orthodox caliphs.

These places were conquered *ṣulḥan* (by peace), *ʿanwatan* (by compulsion), *amānan* [5] (by the grant of a pledge of security), and *quwwatan* (by force). Each

[1] See article "Sunna" by A. J. Wensinck in *E.I.*

[2] See article "Ḥadīth" by Th. W. Juynboll in *E.I.*

[3] In the Egyptian edition the Arabic equivalent of the English phrase "by restraining it" is given *bi-qadhʿihi*; in the German edition more correctly as *bi-qadʿihi*.

[4] Plural of *mīqāt*. The term is used here to denote the stations where pilgrims are bound to assume the *iḥrām* (state of ritual consecration). The *mawāqīt* are as follows: Dhū al-Ḥulayfah for the pilgrims from al-Madīnah; al-Juḥfah for those from Syria and Egypt; Qarn al-Manāzil for those from Najd; Yalamlam for those from Yaman; and Dhāt al-ʿIrq for those from Iraq. A sixth station, Ibrāhīm Mursīa, has been added for the benefit of pilgrims from India and the Far East. These stations are also known as *mahāll,* i.e., the places where the *ihlāl* begins. The term *mawāqīt* is also used to refer to the times of prayer. In the Qur'ān it occurs frequently in the sense of appointed or exact time. See articles "Mīkāt" and "Iḥrām" by A. J. Wensinck in *E.I.*, and Hughes, *Dictionary of Islam,* under "*mīqāt.*"

[5] See article "Amān" by Th. Juynboll in *E.I.*; Majid Khadduri, *The Law of War and*

of these [methods of conquest] has a legal provision in the *sharīʿah* [1] (Muslim law), with regard to the division of *fay'* (property taken from the enemy without fighting), the collection of *jizyah* [2] (poll tax), the levying of *kharāj* (land tax), the gathering of proceeds from *muqāṭaʿāt* (land concessions) and from *muṣālaḥāt* (lands annexed after a peaceful settlement), and the granting of *taswīfāt*, [3] and *iqṭāʿāt* (fiefs).

Jurists cannot afford to remain ignorant of the legal provisions in question, while the princes and the leaders of the Muslim community cannot escape censure if, when journeying along the path of knowledge, they miss the peaks and the plains thereof. For such knowledge constitutes one of the concomitants to judicial decisions and one of the governing rules of Islam and of Muslims.

As regards the compilers of the *siyar*, [4] the *akhbār*, the *ḥadīth*, the *āthār*, and *tawārīkh* (chronicles), their need for a knowledge of geography is greater than the need of gardens for water after the stars have failed to fulfill their promise of rain, and more urgent than the need of the convalescent for health after having despaired of recovery. Geography is the mainstay of their knowledge, for rarely is a leaf, a page, or even a line [5] of their books without it.

As regards men of wisdom, the expositors of knowledge, and those engaged in the practice of medicine and the art of astrology, their need to know geography is no less than the need of those we have referred to above. Physicians have to master it in order to know the humors and airs of countries, astrologers in order to acquaint themselves with the rising and the setting of the stars. For the latter do not pass judgment on countries save by their horoscopes, nor do they

Peace in Islam, (London, 1940), pp. 78-81; Nicolas P. Aghnides, *Mohammedan Theories of Finance*, (New York, 1916,) pp. 355-357.

1 See H. A. R. Gibb, *Mohammedanism*, (London, 1949), pp. 88-106, and article "Sharīʿa" by J. Schacht in *E.I.*

2 See article "Djizya" by C. H. Becker in *E.I.*, and D. C. Dennett, *Conversion and the Poll Tax in Early Islam*, (Cambridge, 1950), *passim*.

3 Dozy refers to the above passage of Yāqūt and gives the following quotation from *Description de l'Egypte*, XI, 498, by way of a definition of *taswīfāt*: "droit prélevé sur le mal el hourr et destiné pour les troupes." See his *Supplément aux Dictionnaires Arabes*, (Leyden, 1881), under "*taswīf*." Al-Jawhari states that the verb *sawwafa* has the meaning of complete delegation of authority, but gives no definition of *taswīfāt*. See his *Ṣiḥāḥ*, under "*sawafa*." Although the term appears as *taswīfāt* in both the German and Egyptian editions of the *Muʿjam*, the possibility that it is merely a misreading of *taswīghāt* should not be overlooked. *Taswīghāt* is derived from the verb *sawwagha*, which means to render a thing permissible, and is often found in the form *taswīghāt aṣ-ṣalāṭīn* (benefits accruing through the sovereign's permission). According to aṣ-Ṣāghāni, as quoted in *Tāj al-ʿArūs*, the latter term is post-classical (*muwalladah*) and signifies the permission granted by the sovereign to take that which is one's due on a particular account, with a view to facilitating things for the taker. See entry "*sawagha*" in *Tāj al-ʿArūs*, in Lane's *Lexicon*, and in al-Fīrūzābādi's *al-Qāmūs al-Muḥīṭ*. In the words of al-Bustāni, *taswīghāt as-salāṭīn* means the conferring of provincial posts by the king. See al-Bustāni, *Muḥīṭ al-Muḥīṭ*, under "sawagha." On the other hand, al-Khwārizmi, one of the earliest writers to define this term, states that it signifies granting a man an exemption from part of his *kharāj* for a given year. See al-Kātib al-Khwārizmi, *Mafātīḥ al-ʿUlūm*, ed. G. Van Vloten, (Leyden, 1895), p. 60. Cf. Dozy, *Supplément aux Dictionnaires Arabes*, under "sawagha."

4 Sing. *sīrah*. The biography of the Prophet; also, biography in general. The plural form *siyar* appears to have been used at an early period in connection with the biography of the Prophet. It was probably because of this that the term *siyar* came to be associated with the term *maghāzi* (military expeditions). Perhaps it is due to this fact that *siyar* books treat of *jihād* (holy war). For further details, see article "Sīra" by G. Levi della Vida in *E.I.*

5 In the Egyptian edition (M.I.), *shaṭr*; in the Egyptian and German editions more correctly *saṭr*.

praise or condemn them without knowing their climes and locations. A mark of perfection of the practicing physician is his desire to know the humors and airs of countries and the salubrity or insalubrity of their soil and water. Thus to these men the mastery of this knowledge has come to be imperative, and the unveiling of its real nature, a philosophical necessity. For this reason many of the ancients composed books which they called *Juqhrāfiyah* (geography), meaning "the image of the earth." Others such as Galen, and Hippocrates before him, wrote books on the humors and airs of countries.

As regards men of letters, it is hardly necessary to emphasize their need for geography. For it constitutes one of the canons and tools [1] of the lexicologist, and provides one of the supports and illustrative examples of the grammarian. It is the mainstay of the poet, who adorns the throat of his poetry with its mention and embellishes the pearl necklaces of his verse with its gold beads. For poetry is not pleasing, nor is the soul of the listener moved by yearning, until the poet mentions Ḥājir, [2] Zarūd, [3] ad-Dahnā', [4] and Habbūd, [5] and expresses longing for the sands of Raḍwa. [6] Thus it becomes incumbent upon the poet to use a place name correctly, give its etymology, determine its location, and describe its meadows and wastelands, highlands (*ḥazns*) [7] and plains. For if he alleges that it is a valley and it turns out to be a mountain, a mountain and it turns out to be a desert, a desert and it turns out to be a river, a river and it turns out to be a village,

[1] Owing to a typographical error the Arabic word *lawāzimihi,* which is the equivalent of the English phrase "his tools", is misspelled in the Egyptian edition.

[2] The name of a place in the lands of Banu Tamīm. See Abu ʿUbayd al-Bakri, *Muʿjam ma Istaʿjam min Asmāʾ al-Biqāʿ*, (Göttingen, 1876), I, 269. However, although this word appears as Ḥājir in both the German and Egyptian editions, it probably should be restored to *ḥajr*. For in the *Muʿjam,* the word *ḥājir* appears not as a place-name but as a land feature, which Yāqūt defines as follows: "*al-ḥājir* in the language of the Arabs is that which keeps water from spilling over the edge of a valley." (Yāqūt, *Muʿjam,* II, 182.) Moreover, under the entry "Ḥajr," Yāqūt gives a detailed account of a town by that name, and at one point speaks of it in words similar to those used in the text above: "Poets have often mentioned it and expressed yearning for it." (*Ibid.*, p. 210.) Ḥajr was the principal town of al-Yamāmah. See *ibid.*, pp. 208-212; al-Ḥasan ibn Aḥmad al-Hamadāni, *Ṣifat Jazīrat al-ʿArab,* ed. D. H. Müller, (Leyden, 1884), I, 161; *Tāj al-ʿArūs,* under "Ḥajr." Ar-Riyāḍ, the modern capital of Saudi Arabia, now stands on the site of Ḥajr. Some old ruins within the confines of this city are still known as "Ḥajr al-Yamāmah." See article "al-Riyāḍ" by A. Grohmann in *E. I. Supplement.*

[3] Region of sands near ath-Thaʿlabīyah, between al-Kūfah and Mecca on the pilgrim road. This place is celebrated in Arab annals because two battles that are reckoned among the *Ayyām al-ʿArab* (the Battles of the Arabs) were fought here. In the First Battle of Zarūd (*Yawm Zarūd al-Awwal*) between the tribes of Bakr and ʿAbs, the former were victorious; in the Second Battle of Zarūd (*Yawm Zarūd ath-Thāni*) between Tamīm and Taghlib, the latter were defeated. See Yāqūt, *Muʿjam,* II, 928, and al-Bakri, *Muʿjam ma Istaʿjam,* I, 436.

[4] "The red," so called from the color of its sands. This is the great desert of Arabia, stretching from the district of al-Ḥarīq to the confines of the Yaman and Ḥaḍramawt. See article "Dahnā" by A. S. Fulton in *E. I.* See also entry "ad-Dahnā," *Muʿjam,* II, 635-636, where Yāqūt gives a very favorable account of this region.

[5] The name of a body of water in the country of the Banu Tamīm; a salty spring in al-Yamāmah; or a mountain. See Yāqūt, *Muʿjam,* IV, 950-951; al-Bakri, *Muʿjam ma Istaʿjam,* II, 826; and *Tāj al-ʿArūs,* under "Habbūd."

[6] A range of hills in Southwestern Arabia, a day's journey from Yanbuʿ. It lies on the right side of the road to al-Madīnah, and on the left side of the road to Mecca. See Yāqūt, *Muʿjam,* II, 790; and article "Raḍwa" by A. Grohmann in *E. I.*

[7] A hard tract of land; high rugged ground. Some *ḥazns,* such as the *ḥazn* of the Banu Yarbūʿ of the Tamīm tribe, are noted for their pasturage. See Yāqūt, *Muʿjam,* II, 260-261, and Lane's *Lexicon,* under "ḥazn."

a village and it turns out to be a *shiʿb*, [1] a *shiʿb* and it turns out to be a *ḥazm*, [2] a *ḥazm* and it turns out to be a *rawḍah*, [3] a *rawḍah* and it turns out to be a *ṣafṣaf*, [4] a *ṣafṣaf* and it turns out to be a swamp, a swamp and it turns out to be a stony region, a stony region and it turns out to be a *sabkhah*, [5] a *sabkhah* and it turns out to be *ḥarrah*, [6] a *ḥarrah* and it turns out to be a plain, a plain and it turns out to be a rocky ground,—or if he locates it in the East and it is in the West, or in the South and it is in the North,—his prestige is lowered and his abundant munificence is diminished. He becomes a laughing-stock and realizes that he is one; he becomes a subject of ridicule and knows that he is one. He is made light of and is regarded with contempt, his beneficence is belittled, and he is deemed an ignoramus.

Some men of learning have said they inferred that the following verse:

> In the gorge below Salʿ [7] lies a murdered man,
> Whose blood shall not go unavenged. [8]

is not of the poetry of Taʾabbaṭa Sharran [9] because there is no gorge below Salʿ.

In our time, a venerable *imām* among men of letters—a noble *shaykh* upon whom there is reliance and to whom recourse is made for the solution of problems—has written a book on the interpretation of the *Maqāmāt* (*Assemblies*), which were composed by Abu Muḥammad al-Qāsim ibn ʿAli ibn Muḥammad al-Ḥarīri. [10] This *imām* achieved complete success in interpreting the diversified synonyms found therein, outstripping everyone who had devoted himself to the explanation of its rare and intricate words. He dazzled minds and astounded intellects by enumerating the secrets of its eloquence, revealing its concealed perfections, elucidating its hidden meanings, manifesting its elegant expressions, and pointing out those words that are alike in form and those that are the choicest and the most excellent.

The public was unanimous in acclaiming the book and agreed that the work

[1] A water-course that flows in a bed flanked by two high banks; a mountain road; a gap or a ravine between two mountains. See Yāqūt, *Muʿjam*, III, 294-296, and Lane's *Lexicon*, under "shiʿb."

[2] Ground that is more elevated than that termed *ḥazn*; a tract of land that is hard and stony, and is so high that men and camels can ascend it only with much effort. See Yāqūt, *Muʿjam*, II, 256-260, and Lane's *Lexicon*, under "ḥazm."

[3] A tract of land with abundant water and lush vegetation; a garden. See Yāqūt, *Muʿjam*, II, 842-860, and Lane's *Lexicon*, under "rawḍah."

[4] A level or even tract of land; a smooth land with no herbage. See Lane's *Lexicon*, under "ṣafṣaf."

[5] A tract of salt land through which water seeps. See Yāqūt, *Muʿjam*, III, 30, and Lane's *Lexicon*, under "sabkhah."

[6] A basalt desert; a volcanic tract of land where the stones are black, worn and crumbling, as though burnt by fire. The general area where the *ḥarrah*-lands occur is between al-Madīnah and Syria. See unsigned article "Ḥarra" in *E.,I*; Yāqūt, Muʿjam, II, 247; O. Loth, "Die Vulkanregionen (Ḥarra's) von Arabien nach Yāḳūt," *ZDMG*, XXII, 365-382; Lane's *Lexicon*, under "ḥarrah."

[7] A mountain near al-Madīnah. See Yāqūt, *Muʿjam*, III, 117-118.

[8] See al-Jawhari, *Ṣiḥāḥ*, under "Salʿ"; Abu Tammām, *Dīwān al-Ḥamāsah*, with interpretation by Abu Zakarīyā Yaḥya ibn ʿAli at-Tabrīzi, (Cairo, A. H. 1926), II, 160 and Charles James Lyall, *Translations of Ancient Arabic Poetry*, (London, 1885), p. 48.

[9] Nickname of a pre-Islamic poet and Bedouin hero, Thābit ibn Jābir ibn Sufyān of the tribe of Fahm. See article "Taʾabbaṭa Sharran" by H. H. Brau in *E. I.*

[10] Grammarian and man of letters, A. H. 446—A. H. 516. His *Maqāmāt*, with a commentary, was published in Paris in 1847 by Silvestre De Sacy. See article "Ḥarīrī" by D. S. Margoliouth in *E. I.*

was excellent in its total effect and in its detail, in the cogency of its facts and in the logic of its reasoning. Copies of the book journeyed far and wide, like the journeying of the sun after sunrise. No daring quibbler or recriminating assailant ventured to reproach him regarding anything contained therein, and no one entertained the idea of undoing the well-knit strands of his meanings, until he mentioned the names of places upon which Abu Muḥammad had based his *Maqāmāt.* Thereupon the thread of his pearl necklace was snapped, the edifice which his beneficence had raised collapsed, his blooming garden dried up, his erstwhile munificence was dissipated, the cavalcade of his virtues lagged, and the perfect body of his work lay prostrate. He became in turn delirious and confused, and began to stumble and grope in the darkness of ignorance.

For example, in commenting upon "The Assembly of Karaj" (*al-Maqāmah al-Karajīyah*) the author said, "Karaj is a town between Hamadān and Adharbayjān"; whereas it actually is a town between Hamadān and Iṣbahān. For the traveler from Hamadān to Iṣbahān takes the road that lies to the southeast, while the traveler from Hamadān to Adharbayjān takes the road that lies to the northwest. The traveler bound for the one turns his back to him who is bound for the other.

Commenting upon "The Assembly of Barqaʿīd" (*al-Barqaʿīdīyah*), he said, "Barqaʿīd is the *qaṣabah* (principal town) of al-Jazīrah"; whereas Barqaʿīd is one of the villages of the *baqʿāʾ* [1] of Mosul, and is scarcely a town, to say nothing of being a principal city.

Commenting upon "The Assembly of Tabrīz" (*at-Tabrīzīyah*), he said, "Tabrīz is one of the *ʿawāṣim* [2] of Syria, and between it and Manbij (Hierapolis) there are twenty *farsakhs*"; whereas Tabrīz is a town too renowned and too outstanding to be thus confounded. Today it is the principal town of the province of Adharbayjān and the most illustrious of its cities.

Because of these and similar errors [which he copied] from others, this *imām* became a laughing stock for idlers and a jest for scoffers, and the detractor found a means of assailing him. Considering his great benevolence, however, these [errors] were of but little consequence. Had he had a [geography] book to which he might have turned, a refuge to which he might have repaired, he would have escaped this misfortune unscathed. He thus would have climbed to a place of eminence instead of slipping into this abyss.

One of the primary motives for the compilation of this book was the fact that at Marv ash-Shāhijān [3] in the year A.H. 615 [A.D. 1218-19], at the salon of our *shaykh,*—the *imām* of happy memory, the martyr Fakhr ad-Dīn Abu al-Muẓaffar ʿAbd ar-Raḥīm, son of the *imām* al-Ḥāfiẓ Tāj al-Islām Abu Saʿd ʿAbd al-Karīm as-Samʿāni, [4]—I was asked about "Ḥubāshah", which is a place mentioned in

[1] Baqʿāʾ is a large *kūrah* between Mosul and Naṣībīn. Barqaʿīd is its principal town. See Yāqūt, *Muʿjam,* I, 701.

[2] An inner ring of fortresses along the Byzantine-Arab frontier. See article "al-ʿAwāṣim" by M. Streck in *E. I.*

[3] The flourishing state of the libraries in Merv indicates that that unfortunate city was enjoying a period of prosperity just before being overwhelmed by the Mongols. For more details on the history of Merv, see article "Merv-ash-Shāhī-Jān" by A. Jakoubonsky in *E. I. Supplement.*

[4] Traditionist and geneologist, A. H. 506/A.D. 1113—A.H. 562/A.D. 1167. Author of *Kitāb al-Ansāb.* See *G.A.L.*, I, 329.

the *ḥadīth* [1] of the Prophet and the site of one of the fairs [2] of the Arabs in the *Jāhilīyah* (Period of Ignorance). I replied:

> I think that it is 'Ḥubāshah' with a *dammah* over the letter 'ḥ', in view of the origin of this word in the [Arabic] language. For *'al-ḥubāshah'* means a group of people from various tribes, and [the expression] *'ḥabashtu lahu ḥubāshah'* means 'I gathered something for him.'

But a narrator of the *ḥadīth* spoke out, saying: "Rather, it is 'Ḥabāshah' with a *fatḥah* over the letter 'ḥ'." He insisted upon his viewpoint, arguing brazenly, displaying obstinacy, and disputing without proof.

I wanted to put an end to this controversy with the aid of traditional knowledge, for in such instances there is no reliance upon etymology or reasoning. Despite all efforts, I failed to find this information in the books of rare *ḥadīths* and lexicographic compilations. This was so despite the adequacy of the books that were to be found in Marv at that time, their accessibility, and their availability for purposes of research. I succeeded in obtaining this information only after the dispute and contention had ceased and after I had despaired of finding it through research and intensive reading. It was, praise be to God, in conformity with that which I had maintained and in agreement with that which I had advocated.

I then became convinced of the need of the world for an accurate book on the subject [of geography], wherein the correct forms of words would be established by the careful transcription of vowel signs, in order that it might be a guide in such darkness and a summoner to the light of that which is correct. I was directed to this noble virtue and my heart was gladdened by the attainment of this glorious [3] honor, which those who had gone before had overlooked, and to which those who came after them had not been guided.

> Says he upon whose ears it falls,
> What has the first left to the last? [4]

How excellent is that which Abu ʿUthmān [al-Jāḥiz] [5] has said:

> Nothing is more detrimental to learning than the saying, 'The first has left nothing to the last,' for it thwarts ambition and diminishes strength. [6]

[1] This is in reference to a report made to the Prophet by one of his followers: "Quraysh has gathered great throngs against you. They have gathered against you a great multitude from various tribes (*Jamaʿu laka al-aḥābīsh*)." See al-Bukhāri, *Ṣaḥīḥ*, III, 116. The term *aḥābīsh* was used to denote the various tribal groups which came together to join Quraysh as allies against the Prophet. It has been said that these tribes were so called because they got together and declared their alliance at the foot of a mountain known as Ḥubshi, or, according to another version, in a valley below Mecca known by that name. See Majd ad-Dīn Muḥammad ibn al-Athīr, *Kitāb an-Nihāyah fi Gharīb al-Ḥadīth w-al-Athar*, (Cairo, A.H. 1311), I, 196; al-Qāḍi ʿIyāḍ, *Kitāb Mashāriq al-Anwār ʿala Ṣiḥāḥ al-Āthār*, (Fās, Morocco, A.H. 1328), I, 176; Yāqūt, *Muʿjam*, II, 197; and al-Khwārizmi, *Mafātīḥ al-ʿUlūm*, p. 127.

[2] A well known fair held in the vicinity of Mecca. The Companion Ḥakīm ibn Ḥizām reports having seen the Prophet there. See al-Bakri, *Muʿjam ma Istaʿjam*, I, 264.

[3] This adjective (*al-jalīlah*) appears in the Egyptian edition, but not in the German edition.

[4] This verse is by Abu Tammām. *Diwān Abi Tammām aṭ-Ṭāʾi*, ed. M. al-Khayyāṭ (Beirut, n.d.), p. 143.

[5] ʿAmr ibn Baḥr. Encyclopedist and man of letters, died A.H. 255/A.D. 869. See *G.A.L.*, I, 152 and *G.A.L. Supplement*, I, 239, 421. See article "al-Djāḥiẓ" (unsigned) in *E.I.*

[6] Wüstenfeld ("Anmerkungen," *Muʿjam*, V, 1) changes the vowelling of the Arabic word *al-minnah* (benevolence or favor) to read *al-munnah* (strength). This word is unvowelled in the Egyptian edition. The same saying in a slightly different form is attributed by Yāqūt to al-Jāḥiẓ in *Irshād*, ed. Margoliouth, (London, 1913), *G.M.S.*, VI, 58.

Our predecessors, however have written books on the names of places, and we have followed their example and have been guided by them. These books fall into two classes: those that were intended to treat of thriving cities and famed and populous countries; and those that were intended to treat of deserts and wastelands and that were confined to Arab encampments mentioned in the poetry and the lore of the Arabs.

As regards those who have mentioned the inhabited places, they comprise a large group. Among them are a number of the ancients, philosophers and men of wisdom, including Plato, Pythagoras, Ptolemy and many others of this class; they called their books on this subject "Geography", which means "the image of the earth". I have come upon several of their books, but most of the places mentioned therein are unknown to me. The identity of these places remains a mystery to us, for they have fallen into oblivion with the passage of time and are now beyond recognition. Islamic writers constitute another category. They pursued a course close to those mentioned above in describing cities and kingdoms and in determining the distances of routes and highways. These writers include: Ibn Khurradādhbih, [1] Aḥmad ibn Wāḍiḥ, [2] al-Jayhāni, [3] Ibn al-Faqīh, [4] Abu Zayd al-Balkhi, [5] Abu Isḥāq al-Iṣṭakhri, [6] Ibn Ḥawqal, [7] Abu ʿAbd Allāh al-Bashshāri, [8] al-Ḥasan ibn Muḥammad al-Muhallabi [9] Ibn Abu ʿAwn al-Bagh-

[1] Abu al-Qāsim ʿUbayd Allāh ibn ʿAbd Allāh. Geographer, born in the early years of the third century A.H./ninth century A.D. and died *ca.* A.H. 300/A.D. 912-3. See article "ibn Khordādhbeh" by C. Van Arendonk in *E.I.* Cf. *G.A.L.*, I, 225 and *G.A.L. Supplement*, I, 404. The book referred to is *Kitāb al-Masālik w-al-Mamālik, B.G.A.*, VI. It will be noted that the above form of reading this author's name has been adopted in preference to the older form of "Khordadhbeh" and its variants. J. H. Kramers has recommended it as the more correct form. (See his article "Djughrāfiyā" in *E. I. Supplement.*) C. Brockelmann has adopted the form "Ḫorradādbeh" since the first publication of the *G.A.L.* in 1898, while more recently Franz Rosenthal has used the form "Ḫurradādhbih" in his *A History of Muslim Historiography*, (Leyden, 1952).

[2] Al-Kātib al-ʿAbbāsi al-Yaʿqūbi. Historian and geographer, died after A.H. 292/A.D. 905; see *Yaʿḳūbī les pays*, tr. G. Wiet (Cairo, 1937), pp. viii-ix. Cf. article "al-Yaʿḳūbi" by C. Brockelmann in *E. I.*; *G.A.L.*, I, 226-227, and *G.A.L. Supplement*, I, 405.

[3] Abu ʿAbd Allāh Muḥammad ibn Aḥmad. Samanid minister of 10th century A.D. and author of a geographical work entitled *Kitāb al-Masālik w-al-Mamālik*. See *G.A.L.*, I, 228, and *G.A L. Supplement*, I, 407. See also article "Djughrāfiyā" by J. H. Kramers in *E. I. Supplement.*

[4] Abu Bakr Aḥmad ibn Muḥammad ibn Isḥāq al-Hamadhāni, died *circa* A.H. 289/A.D. 902. Geographer and author of *Mukhtaṣar Kitāb al-Buldān, B.G.A.* V, which is a compendium of a larger work. The second half of the original book is thought to be in the Mashhad MS discovered by A. Zeki Validi Togan in 1923. *G.A.L.*, I, 227 and *G.A.L. Supplement*, I, 405; article "Ibn al-Faḳīh" (unsigned) in *E.I.*

[5] Aḥmad ibn Sahl. Geographer, died at the age of 87 in A.H. 322/A.D. 934. See article "al-Balkhī" by Cl. Huart in *E. I.* Cf. *G.A.L. Supplement*, I, 408. Al-Balkhi was author of *Ṣuwar al-Aqālīm* (*The Images of the Climes*), which is believed to have been incorporated into al-Iṣṭakhri's *Kitāb al-Masālik w-al-Mamālik, B.G.A.*, I.

[6] Ibrāhīm ibn Muḥammad al-Fārisi. Geographer of 4th century A.H./10th century A.D. Author of *Kitāb al-Masālik w-al-Mamālik, B.G.A.*, I. See article "al-Iṣṭakhrī" (unsigned) in *E. I.*

[7] Abu al-Qāsim Muḥammad. Geographer and traveller of the 4th century A.H./10th century A.D. Author of *Kitāb Ṣūrat al-Arḍ, B.G.A.* II. See article "ibn Ḥawḳal" by C. van Arendonk in *E. I.* Cf. *G.A.L. Supplement*, I, 408.

[8] Geographer and traveller. Born *circa* A.D. 946; died *circa* A.D. 1000. Author of *Kitāb Aḥsan at-Taqāsīm fi Maʿrifat al-Aqālīm, B.G.A.*, III. About one-half of this work has been translated into English by G.S.A. Ranking and R.F. Azoo under the title *Aḥsanu-t-taqāsīm fi Maʿrifati-l-Aqālīm*, Bibliotheca Indica, (Calcutta, 1897-1910). See *G.A.L.*, I, 230, and *G.A.L. Supplement*, I, 410. It should be pointed out here that while Yāqūt throughout the *Muʿjam* refers to this author as al-Bashshāri, he is also known as al-Muqaddasi or al-Maqdisi.

dādi, [1] and Abu ʿUbayd al-Bakri [al-Andalusi], [2] who is the author of a book called *al-Masālik w-al-Mamālik* (*The Routes and the Kingdoms*).

As regards those who have described Arabian places and Bedouin encampments, this class comprises men of letters. They include: Abu Saʿīd al-Aṣmaʿi, [3] whose work I chanced upon in the form of a narration by Ibn Durayd, [4] who had it from ʿAbd ar-Raḥmān, [5] who had it from his uncle; Abu ʿUbayd as-Sakūni; al-Ḥasan ibn Aḥmad al-Hamadāni, [6] who has a book called *Jazīrat al- ʿArab* (*The Island of the Arabs*); Abu al-Ashʿath al-Kindi, who has a book on the mountains of Tihāmah; Abu Saʿīd as-Sīrāfi, [7] who, I have been informed, has a

Although his *E.I.* article on this author is entitled "al-Muḳaddasi," Kramers makes it quite plain in this article that he regards "al-Maḳdisi" as the preferable form. Other authorities who seem to prefer it include Barthold, Gibb, and Minorsky. See W. Barthold, *Turkestan Down to the Mongol Invasion*, trans. and ed. with the assistance of H.A.R. Gibb, (London, 1928), *passim*; *Ḥūdūd al-ʿĀlam*, trans. and ed. by V. Minorsky, (London, 1937), *passim*; and the *E.I.* (new edition).

[9] Geographer, died A.H. 380. This author's name should read al-Ḥasan ibn Aḥmad (instead of Muḥammad) al-Muhallabi. This error is corrected in the index of proper names of the German edition, *Muʿjam*, VI, 388, but stands uncorrected in the Egyptian edition. Al-Muhallabi was the author of a book entitled *Kitāb al-Masālik w-al-Mamālik*, which he wrote for the Fatimid al-ʿAzīz (Ismāʿīl Pāsha al-Baghdādi erroneously says al-Muʿizz), and which he called *al-Kitāb al-ʿAzīzi* after his name. According to Kramers, only quotations from this work are preserved by Yāqūt and Abu al-Fidā'. See article "Djughrāfiyā" by J. H. Kramers in *E. I. Supplement*; Ḥājji Khalīfah, *Kitāb Kashf aẓ-Ẓunūn ʿan Asāmi al-Kutub w-al-Funūn*, (Istanbul, 1943), II, 1665; Ismāʿīl Pāsha al-Baghdādi, *Hadīyat al-ʿĀrifīn Asmā' al-Mu'allifīn wa-Āthār al-Muṣannifīn*, (Istanbul, 1951), I, 272; and F. Wüstenfeld, "Die Literatur der Erdbeschreibung bei den Arabern", *Zeitschrift für Vergleichende Erdkunde*, (Magdeburg, 1842), no. 31, p. 34.

[1] More properly Abu ʿAwn Isḥāq ibn ʿAli. Very little is known about the man or his work. Nallino thinks that his *zīj* is based upon that of al-Khwārizmi. He points out that 27 out of 30 coordinates attributed by Yāqūt to the *zīj* of Abu ʿAwn seem to derive from al-Khwārizmi's *Kitāb Ṣūrat al-Arḍ*. Nallino refers to the dearth of precise information on this author and points out that his name is not found in any other work. See C. A. Nallino, "Al-Ḫuwārizmi e il suo rifacimento della Geografia di Tolomeo", *Raccolta di Scritti editi e inediti*, (Rome, 1944), V, 488-489. Justus Heer is of the opinion that ibn ʿAwn is either the editor or perhaps merely the copyist of al-Khwārizmi's work. For more details see F. Justus Heer, *Die historischen und geographischen Quellen in Jāqūt's geographischem Wörterbuch*, (Strassburg, 1898), pp. 24-25.

[2] ʿAbd Allāh ibn Muḥammad. Hispano-Arab geographer, died A.H. 487/A.D. 1094. A copy of his *Kitāb al-Masālik w-al-Mamālik*, which at one time was believed to have existed only in fragments, was discovered by Professor Ritter in the library of the Laleli Mosque in Istanbul. See *Der Islam*, (1931) XIX, 57. Parts dealing with North Africa were published by de Slane in 1857, translated in 1858, and ultimately reprinted in Algiers in 1910 as *Description de l'Afrique Septentrionale*. Parts dealing with the Russians and the Slavs were published and translated by Kunik and Baron V. Rosen under the title *Izvestiya al-Bekri i drugikh avtorov o Rusi i Slavyanakh*, (St. Petersburg, 1878). See article "al-Bakrī" by A. Cour in *E. I.* and the more up-to-date article "Abu ʿUbayd al-Bakrī" by E. Lévi-Provençal in *E.I.* (new edition). Cf. *G.A.L.*, I, 476.

[3] ʿAbd al-Malik ibn Qurayb. Lexicologist and man of letters, A.H. 122/A.D. 740—A.H. 213/A.D. 828. See article "al-Aṣmaʿī" by A. Haffner in *E.I.*

[4] Philologist, grammarian and poet, A.H. 223/A.D. 837—A.H. 321/A.D. 933. See article "Ibn Duraid" by J. Pedersen in *E.I.*

[5] Nephew of al-Aṣmaʿi. A writer of the 2nd century A.H. whose reliability as a transmitter from his uncle and other contemporary men of learning is praised by Ibn an-Nadīm. See Muḥammad ibn Isḥāq ibn an-Nadīm, *Kitāb al-Fihrist*, ed. G. Flügel, (Leipzig, 1871) I, 56.

[6] Geographer and historian, died A.H. 334/A.D. 945-6. The book referred to, *Ṣifat Jazīrat al-ʿArab*, was edited by D. H. Müller and published in Leyden in 1884. See articles "al-Hamdānī" by C. van Arendonk in *E.I.* and *E.I. Supplement*.

[7] al-Ḥasan ibn ʿAbd Allāh ibn al-Marzubān, A.H. 280-A.H. 368. See article "Sīrāfī" by F. Krenkow in *E. I.*

book on the island of the Arabs, and Abu Muḥammad al-Aswad al-Ghundijāni, [1] who has a book on the waters of the Arabs. A large portion of the latter book is included in the *Anecdotes* of Abu Ziyād al-Kilābi, [2] most of which I have read. Others in this group whose books I have read are Muḥammad al-Kalbi, [3] who wrote *Manāhil al-ʿArab* (*The Watering Places of the Arabs*), and Hishām ibn Muḥammad al-Kalbi, [4] who wrote *Ishtiqāq al-Buldān* (*The Etymology of Countries*). Then there is Abu al-Qāsim az-Zamakhshari, [5] who has a pleasing book on the same subject; Abu al-Ḥasan al-ʿImrāni, a student of az-Zamakhshari, who studied the book of his master and added to it, and whose work I have seen; Abu ʿUbayd al-Bakri al-Andalusi, who has a book called *Muʿjam ma Istaʿjam min Asmā' al-Biqāʿ* [6] (*The Dictionary of Obscure Place Names*), which I have not been able to find though I have searched for it and inquired about it time and again; and Abu Bakr Muḥammad ibn Mūsa al-Ḥāzimi, [7] who has a book called *Ma Ikhtalaf wa-I'talaf min Asmāʾ al-Biqāʿ* (*Similar and Dissimilar Place Names*).

Later our friend the *ḥāfiẓ* and *imām* Abu ʿAbd Allāh Muḥammad ibn Maḥmūd ibn an-Najjār, [8]—may God reward him well—acquainted me with an abridgement prepared by the *ḥāfiẓ* Abu Mūsa Muḥammad ibn ʿUmar al-Iṣbahāni [9] of a book written by Abu al-Fatḥ Naṣr ibn ʿAbd ar-Raḥmān al-Iskandari, [10] the grammarian, entitled *Fīma Ikhtalaf wa-Iʾtalaf min Asmāʾ al-Biqāʿ* (*On Similar and Dissimilar Place Names*). I found this book to be the work of a meticulous man who had spent a lifetime putting it together and who had excelled in producing a memorial and a work of substance. Thus I found out that al-Ḥāzimi, may God have mercy upon him, had plagiarized it and claimed it as his own, and deeming other scholars ignorant, claimed its authorship. When I first came upon his book I held him in great esteem for his learning and thought that his ability

[1] al-Ḥasan ibn Aḥmad. Geneologist and lexicologist, died A.H. 433. See Yāqūt, *Irshād*, III, 261-265; as-Sūyūṭi, *Bughyat al-Wuʿāh fi Ṭabaqāt al-Lughawīyīn w-an-Nuḥāh*, (Cairo, A.H. 1326); ʿAbd ar-Raḥmān ibn Muḥammad al-Anbāri, *Nuzhat al-Alibbāʾ fi Ṭabaqāt al-Udabāʾ*, (Cairo, n.d.), p. 437. In the Egyptian edition the name of this author is vocalized as al-Ghundajāni, but in the German edition it is vocalized as al-Ghundijāni, as in Yāqūt's *Irshād*.

[2] Yazīd ibn ʿAbd Allāh ibn al-Ḥurr. Poet of the 2nd century A.H. His *Kitāb an-Nawādir* is listed by ibn an-Nadīm, *al-Fihrist*, I, 44.

[3] Historian and philologist, died A.H. 146/A.D. 763. See article "al-Kalbī" by C. Brockelmann in *E.I.*

[4] Historian and philologist, son of the foregoing. Died A.H. 204/A.D. 819 (or A.H. 206). See article "al-Kalbī" by C. Brockelmann in *E.I.*

[5] Muḥammad ibn ʿUmar. Scholar, theologian, and philologist, A.H. 467/A.D. 1075—A.H. 538/A.D. 1144. See article "al-Zamakhsharī "by C. Brockelmann in *E.I.* The book referred to is *Kitāb al-Jibāl w-al-Amkinah w-al-Miyāh*, ed. Saverda de Grave, (Leyden, 1855); second edition published by al-Maṭbaʿah al-Ḥaydarīyah of Najaf, Iraq, in A.H. 1357.

[6] Yāqūt often cites this work in the *Muʿjam* through secondary sources. It is now available in two editions: ed. F. Wüstenfeld, (Göttingen, 1876), 2 vols; ed. Muṣṭafa as-Saqqā, (Cairo, 1945), 3 vols.

[7] Traditionist, died A.H. 584/A.D. 1188. The book referred to is *al-Muʾtalif w-al-Mukhtalif fi Asmāʾ al-Buldān*. See adh-Dhahabi, *Tadhkirat al-Ḥuffāẓ*, (Ḥaydarābād, A.H. 1334), IV, 151-153; *G.A.L.*, I, 356 and *G.A.L. Supplement*, I, 605.

[8] Historian and traditionist, A.H. 578/A.D. 1183—A.H. 643/A.D. 1245. See *G.A.L.*, I, 360, and *G.A.L. Supplement*, I, 613.

[9] Traditionist, A.H. 501/A.D. 1108—A.H. 581/A.D. 1185. See *G.A.L.*, I, 365, and *G.A.L. Supplement*, I, 625.

[10] Grammarian and writer on geography, died A.H. 561. The book referred to may be *Kitāb fi Asmāʾ al-Buldān w-al-Amkinah w-al-Miyāh*, which as-Suyūṭi attributes to him. See as-Suyūṭi, *Bughyat al-Wuʿāh*, p. 403.

was greater than the task to which he had addressed himself. But God unmasked his true nature, and the pure milk was separated from the scum.

As for me, everything that I have copied from the book of Naṣr (ibn ʿAbd ar-Raḥmān al-Iskandari) I have attributed to him and acknowledged as his. I have not deprived him of [the fruits of] his labors, neither have I dimmed his fame nor dissipated his efforts. May God recompense him and have mercy upon him!

These are the books that have been written on this subject and from which I have copied. I have also copied from the anthologies of poetry of the [ancient] Arabs and of the Moderns; from the chronicles of men of letters and the transmitters of *ḥadīth*; from the mouths of narrators, and from sundry books. But that which I have observed in my travels and gleaned in my wanderings far exceeds what I obtained from these sources. God is the cause of success, if He so wills.

As regards the first category of writers, place names occurring in their books are altered, changed, and relegated to oblivion, having been distorted by those who copied them down. Books written by the second category of writers, though based upon accurate principles and carefully transcribed by men of learning, are not well organized and therefore are not conducive to the satisfaction of the inquirer because they are excessively abridged, unvoweled and dismembered. For the aim of these writers is to establish the correct forms of words, and not to search for changes occurring therein or to elucidate other matters.

Thus I sought the guidance of God the Most High (*istakhartu Allāh taʿāla* [1]), gathered that which they had scattered, and added to it that which they had overlooked. I arranged [my book] in alphabetical order and composed it in the precise manner of the lexicologists, indicating whether each letter in a given place name is voweled or unvoweled, thus removing from it the element of ambiguity. I thereby turned into gold that which had been but brass.

I have endeavored to give the etymology of a place name, if it be Arabic; its meaning, if it be foreign; and, if I happen to know it, the clime wherein it is located, its horoscope, and the stars which govern it; the names of its founders, famous towns lying near it, and the distances between it and neighboring towns; its distinctive features and the wonderful things associated with it; some of the notables, the pious men, the Companions, and the Followers buried therein; lines of poetry expressing yearning for one's native land which were inspired by it and which serve as evidence [2] of the correctness and accuracy of its name; the time when it was conquered by the Muslims, the manner in which this came about, the name of its ruler at the time, and whether it was conquered by peace treaty (*ṣulḥan*) or by compulsion (*ʿanwatan*), so that you might know its status with regard to *fay'* and *jizyah*, and who holds dominion over it in our time.

It is not possible for us, however, to fulfill these conditions with regard to

[1] This term signifies the prayer of a person seeking divine guidance to enable him to make up his mind regarding any contemplated undertaking. Authors often use it in introductions to their books. For further details, see article "Istikhāra" by I. Goldziher in *E.I.* It should be pointed out here that Yāqūt makes a rare and perhaps unprecedented use of *istikhārah*. For not only does he turn to God for guidance as he picks up his pen to embark upon the writing of the *Muʿjam*, but he turns to God again before laying it down. In the colophon to the *Muʿjam*, IV, 1047, which is largely an echo of the introduction, he says: "I have sought guidance from God the Most High (*istakhartu Allāh taʿāla*), He who is possessed of power and might, and stopped here, etc." Goldziher, in the above-mentioned article, cites no parallel to the use Yāqūt has made of this formula.

[2] In the Egyptian edition, *ash-shāhid*; in the German edition, more correctly *ash-shāhidah*.

everything we shall mention, nor is it within the power of anyone else to do so. For such information is available only in the case of famous cities and flourishing metropolises. Some of these conditions, but not others, may have been adequately met as a result of that which we have arrived at through investigation and obtained through travel and inquiry.

Thus I have procured for you all or most of the benefits of this knowledge and have bestowed upon you the mastery thereof, with no effort on your part. I have even mentioned many things which the intellect rejects and against which the nature of a cultured man revolts, because they are far removed from prevailing customs and at variance with commonly observed usages. Nothing, however, should be deemed too great, considering the power of the Creator and the cunning of the creature. I myself view such things with skepticism and shrink from them, and I wish to disavow to the reader any responsibility for their authenticity. I have included them merely out of a desire to obtain whatever benefits may be obtained therefrom and to acquire whatever necklaces and rare jewels of knowledge they may contain. If these accounts be true, we shall have had the good fortune of one who has been right; if they be false, they still partake of truth, for I copied them as I found them. I have been truthful in reporting them as I have done, in order that you may know what has been said concerning them, whether they be true or false. For if someone says, "I heard Zayd lie," you would want to know the manner in which he lied.

Behold the leaders among the *ḥāfiẓs,* who are the models to be emulated in every age, and upon whom there is reliance with respect to obligations imposed by the *sharʿ* (divine law) and by the *sunan* (practices of the Prophet). The majority of the *ḥāfiẓs* in their *musnads*—which comprise the *ḥadīths* of the Apostle, upon which legal provisions are based and by means of which *ḥalāl* (that which is permitted) is differentiated from *ḥarām* (that which is forbidden)—have not stipulated the inclusion of the *ṣaḥīḥ* (sound) *ḥadīths* and the exclusion of the *saqīm* (unsound) *ḥadīths,* or the negation of the *muʿwaj* (irregular) *ḥadīths* and the confirmation of the *mustaqīm* (regular) *ḥadīths.* This fact has not precluded these *ḥāfiẓs* from being reckoned among men of truthfulness, nor has it caused them to be ejected from the ranks of the *imāms* or from Islam. They related what they heard, as their memories had retained it. For he is called a liar who fabricates a *ḥadīth,* or transmits it from a person from whom he has not heard it, or transmits it from a person whom he has not previously used as a source. If, however, he narrates that which he has heard as he heard it, he is reckoned among the truthful, and the responsibility rests upon him from whom he received it. However, if he be one of those entitled to exercise his own judgment, he may narrate it and pronounce it to be spurious. [1] Were it not so, many of the *ḥadīths* would have been nullified. It is therefore incumbent upon us to follow the example of the *ḥāfiẓs* and hold fast to their rope.

A fact that can neither be denied by a man of keen intelligence nor contradicted by a man of mature judgment is that the obstinate disputant wearies both himself and others, whereas the fair-minded person enjoys peace of mind and imparts it to others. What man has been granted infallibility and has come to know every word? Yet he who seeks knowledge shall find it. I admit that even after

[1] In the German edition, *yuzayyighahu*; in the Egyptian edition, more correctly *yuzayyifahu.*

exerting my faculties to the utmost, I am capable of erring and falling short of the attainment of what is right. Therefore, let him who would demand infallibility of us seek it first for himself. If it eludes him, he will have supported our contention, and in this he will be right. However, if he alleges that he has attained infallibility, he will then have proved that he is not one of those capable of open-minded discussion.

As the years went by while this book was being put together, and the days and months followed one another while the knowledge contained therein was being acquired, I did not reach a goal that satisfied me; nor did I, despite repeated attempts, stop at a certain point and say, "This is it!" I saw the moon of the night of youth trip over [1] the train of the eclipsed sun of old age and take to flight, and watched the spring of life enter upon the summer of its expiration, accompanied by the signs of senility and death.

I stopped at this point, hoping to fulfill a lifelong ambition by presenting the book to the reader before passing away. Fearing the suddenness of death, I hastened to produce the book without delay. For I am exceedingly apprehensive of being overwhelmed by the night of death before the dawn of this book breaks upon the world. Since no one has urged me to write it or has expressed an interest in it, I await the forces of discouragement. For what confidence can I have in the army of life, which has been attacked at night by hosts of mysterious diseases, as by predatory wolves? Or what faith can I have in the arrival of morning, following a night during which I was thwarted by obstacles at every turn?

Notwithstanding all this, I declare—and I am not abashed to do so, and I challenge every eminent man of learning to combat, from which I shall not flee—that this book is unique in its field and exalted above its peers. No one is capable of producing its like, save him who has been favored with success and has journeyed along every highway in search of the knowledge contained therein, descending at times, ascending at others, risking his life for its sake, and venturing far. No one can do so but him who has dedicated himself to it in the season of youth and its fervor, who has been helped by the length and sufficiency of life, and who has manifested the signs of eagerness and its vigor. Indeed, though I were to belittle this goal, it is great, and though I were to minimize it, I swear by the eternal God, it is manifold.

With regard to the comprehension of all knowledge, this is a matter which is impossible of attainment within a lifetime, and which is precluded by the twin obstacles of old age and death. [2] I have therefore cut short my investigations, despite a surging zeal and an aspiring eye that has ever sought more knowledge. Had I been able to rely upon the advantage of a long life and to feel confident of success because of the adequacy of its length and the hopes I pinned upon it, I should have increased the volume of my book many fold and added to it hundreds, even thousands, of other benefits.

Had I sought the wide circulation of this book and aimed at the spread of its name and renown, I should have abridged it in a manner commensurate with the

[1] In the German edition, *taʿashshur*; in the Egyptian edition, more correctly *taʿaththur*.

[2] In the Egyptian edition, *ma naʿa* (that which announces death); in the German edition, more correctly *mānīʿā* (the twin obstacles). Wüstenfeld translates and explains this phrase as "'die beiden Hindernisse des Unvermögens und Unterganges' d.h. Altersschwäche und Tod." See "Anmerkungen," *Muʿjam*, V, 509.

ambitions of these times and with the limited aspirations of contemporary seekers of knowledge. But I allowed myself to be led by my insatiable desire [for knowledge] and to be dragged by the halter of eagerness to that which has motivated my ambition.

I besought God, might and majesty to Him, not to deny me the recompense for my labors in writing this book and not to abandon me to my own devices in whatsoever I might resolve upon and undertake. My reward for that towards which I have spurred the procession of my thoughts, and in the attainment of which I have deprived my body and my eyes of sleep, lies in charitable mention by the faithful, and in the prayers of those who benefit [from my book] that I be included in the company of the righteous on the Day of Judgment.

Students have oftentimes requested me to abridge this book, but I have steadfastly refused to do so. Because of their petty ambitions, I found among them neither patrons nor supporters; yet I yielded not to them, nor was I turned away from my purpose.

I enjoin him who copies this book, as well as him who benefits from it, not to waste my labors or disregard the spirit of dedication in which I undertook this task by abridging or condensing it. For in so doing he would be squandering that which I have gathered and scattering that which I have put together; he would be dispersing the accumulated virtues of the book and negating every precious element of its substance and its concealed merits; he would be divesting its neck of its ornaments and glittering gems and usurping the manifestation of its secrets and benefits. For often he who shuns the word of another covets it, and he who is indifferent to[1] the witticism of another is enamored of it and exhausts his mount in pursuing it.

Thus if you comply with my wishes, you will be doing your duty toward me, may God include you among the righteous; however, if you fail to do so, you will be guilty of being undutiful toward me, may God be your reckoner in the ultimate abode.

Know, then, that he who condenses a book is like one who comes upon a comely person and cuts off his limbs, leaving him with maimed hands and crippled legs, blinded eyes and severed ears, or like one who robs a knight in armor of his weapons, leaving him unarmed and unhorsed.

It has been related that al-Jāḥiẓ composed a book which he divided into chapters and that it was dismembered by a contemporary of his who deleted parts of it. Al-Jāḥiẓ called him into his presence and said to him.:

> Behold, O you, the author is like a painter. In my book I have painted a portrait that had two eyes, and you blinded them—may God blind your eyes! It had two ears, and you severed them—may God sever your ears! It had two hands, and you cut them off—may God cut off your hands . . ."

Al-Jāḥiẓ went on in this manner, enumerating the other features of the portrait. Thereupon the man apologized for being so ignorant and expressed his repentance, pledging not to resort to such practices again.

I have presented this copy, done in my own hand, to the library of our master, —the distinguished statesman, the great and venerable man of learning, he who is of surpassing beneficence and widespread favors, of noble lineage and ancient

[1] In the German edition, *zāhid ʿan*; in the Egyptian edition, more correctly *zāhid fī*.

glory, of unshakable power and towering rank, he who has attained perfection of character, who wears noble qualities like a bejeweled sword, the leader of benevolent men, the first among ministers, the grandest and most illustrious lord,—the judge Abu al-Ḥasan ʿAli ibn Yūsuf ibn Ibrāhīm ibn ʿAbd al-Wāḥid ash-Shaybāni at-Taymi. [1] May God preserve his glory, cover him [2] with His shadow, destroy his equal, grant victory to his troops, and put his opponent to flight.

For ever since I set upon my travels and found myself engaged in dueling with Fate and parrying its thrusts, whenever I applied to him for help, he unfailingly bestowed upon me a portion of his wealth and,

> When my traveling was done and I had reached the journey's end
> After what I had experienced of hardship and of ease,

after suffering long the scorching [3] of misfortune and waiting for the light of good luck to break through the curtained darkness enveloping it,

> I grasped one of Ibn Yūsuf's ropes,
> Thus guarding myself against hard times.

He thus protected me from adversity and the vicissitudes of life and set my mind at rest by mitigating the stubbornness of evil times. It was then that:

> I hid myself from Fate beneath the shadow of his wing,
> My eyes beholding Fate, though it beheld me not.

Under his protection I found myself in a secure refuge, and as a result of his beneficence and generosity I came to be in an invulnerable position. Thus,

> If Fate be asked, it would not know of me,
> Nor would it know if asked where I might be. [4]

He was, may God perpetuate his exaltedness, a mountain of learning in our time and the foremost man of our day and age. I have returned to him the benefits I have received from him, and he has spoken of me as I have spoken of him. May God reward him well on my behalf and preserve his power and glory through Muḥammad and his noble family.

By way of a preface to this dictionary, I have written five introductory chapters, through which its benefits are enhanced [5] and its bountifulness increased.

Chapter I treats of the image of the earth, with an account of what the ancients have said regarding its shape and what we have transmitted from the moderns regarding its image.

[1] Abu al-Ḥasan ʿAli ibn Yūsuf al-Qifṭi (called Jamāl ad-Dīn), A.H. 568/A.D. 1172—A.H. 646/A.D. 1248. A synopsis of his *Kitāb Ikhbār al-ʿUlamāʾ bi-Akhbār al-Ḥukamāʾ* by az-Zawzani is called *al-Muntakhabāt al-Multaqaṭāt min Kitāb Taʾrīkh al-Ḥukamāʾ*, ed. Julius Lippert, (Leipzig, 1903). See article "Ibn al-Ḳifṭī" by C. Brockelmann in *E. I.*

[2] In the Egyptian edition (M.I.), *aṣbagha*; in the Egyptian and German editions, more correctly *asbagha*.

[3] This word, which appears erroneously as *ḥurfah* in the Egyptian and German editions, should be restored to *ḥurqah* as in the Egyptian edition (M.I.).

[4] This verse is found in a slightly different form in Ibn Khaldūn, *al-Muqaddimah*, (Cairo, A.H. 1322), I, 13. For a French translation, see *Les Prolégomènes d'Ibn Khaldoun*, trad. M. de Slane, (Paris, 1934), I, 43. See also Taqi ad-Dīn Aḥmad ibn ʿAli al-Maqrīzi, *Ittiʿāẓ al-Ḥunafāʾ bi-Akhbār al-Aʾimmah al-Fāṭimīyīn al-Khulafāʾ*, (Cairo, 1948), p. 64.

[5] In the German edition, *yasummu*; in the Egyptian edition, *yasmu*.

Chapter II treats of differences among writers concerning the definition of the word *iqlīm* (clime), its nature and its etymology, and the means of determining the *qiblah*[1] in every part of the world.

Chapter III treats of the definition of terms recurring in this book, such as *barīd, farsakh, mīl, kūrah,* and the like.

Chapter IV treats of the interpretation of legal provisions governing lands and countries conquered by the Muslims, as well as rules governing the division of *fay'* and *kharāj* in lands conquered by peace treaty or by compulsion.

Chapter V treats of certain accounts of countries. In order to enhance the benefits of this book and enable the reader to dispense with other works on this subject, these accounts have not been confined to any one locality.

I have divided this work into 28 books, one for each of the letters of the alphabet. I then have divided each book into 28 chapters, second letters having been assigned a chapter each, in alphabetical order. In each of these chapters I have followed the procedure of arranging every word according to the first letter, then the second, the third, the fourth, and so on, up to the last letter of the word. I thus have given precedence to that letter to which precedence should be given, in accordance with the order of the letters in the alphabet, i.e., A, B, C, D, etc. I have done so without taking into consideration the root of the word or its augmented forms. For all the words occurring in the text are but singular proper nouns; most of them are non-Arabic and improvised and do not admit of etymological treatment. The purpose of this arrangement is to eliminate difficulties and make the benefits of the book readily accessible.

God is our supporter in that which we have undertaken and our guide in the pursuit of that which we have aimed at, with no power and no might in us save in Him alone.

I have called this book *The Dictionary of Countries,* a name appropriate for the subject. God is sufficient unto us, and He is the best trustee. The fair copy of this work was begun on the night of the twenty-first of Muḥarram in the year A. H. 625 (January 1, 1228).

And of God we ask assistance for its completion through His favors and generosity.

[1] See article "Ḳibla" I and II by A. J. Wensinck and C. Schoy in *E.I.*

CHAPTER I

ON THE DESCRIPTION OF THE EARTH, THE MOUNTAINS, THE SEAS, AND OTHER FEATURES THEREOF

GOD SAID, might and majesty be His, "Have we not made the earth like unto a flat expanse, and the mountains like unto stakes [1]?" He said, might and majesty be His, "It is God who hath made for you the earth an abode, and the heaven a roof [2] . . . . . ." He said, glory be to Him, "And God hath made the earth a carpet for you [3] . . ." The commentators have said that "carpet" and "expanse" signify "abode" and the control and use thereof.

The ancients have disagreed as to the shape and form of the earth. Some of them have stated that it is flat-surfaced and spread out in four directions—in the east and in the west, in the north and in the south. [4] There are among them those who have held that it is shaped like a shield, [5] those who have held that it is shaped like a table, [6] and those who have held that it is shaped like a drum.[7]

[1] Qur'ān LXXVIII, 6-7.

[2] Qur'ān XL, 66.

[3] Qur'ān LXXI, 18.

[4] This statement is almost identical with that found in Aḥmad ibn ʿUmar ibn Rustah, *Kitāb al-Aʿlāq an-Nafīsah, B.G.A.*, VII, 23. See also Zakarīyā ibn Muḥammad al-Qazwīni, *ʿAjāʾib al-Makhlūqāt,* ed. Ferdinand Wüstenfeld, (Göttingen, 1849), p. 144. Cf. Sirāj ad-Dīn Abu Ḥafṣ ʿUmar ibn al-Wardi, *Kharīdat al-ʿAjāʾib wa-Farīdat al-Gharāʾib,* (Cairo, A.H. 1324), p. 10. It should be pointed out here that the content of Chapter I of Ibn al-Wardi's book is based largely on this chapter of Yāqūt's *Muʿjam.* Often the same concepts are treated in both texts in strikingly similar language. In fact, with the exception of some minor variations, Ibn al-Wardi's text reads like a rearrangement, and sometimes like a condensation, of the material found in this chapter. For this reason, it is felt that repeated references to Ibn al-Wardi will be unnecessary, except in certain instances where comparison is called for. According to Moh. Ben Cheneb, Ibn al-Wardi (d. A.D. 1457) plagiarized *Jāmiʿ al-Funūn wa-Salwat al-Maḥzūn* of Najm ad-Dīn Aḥmad ibn Ḥamdān al-Ḥanbali (*ca.* A.D. 1332). See article "Ibn al-Wardī" by M. Ben Cheneb in *E. I.* If Ibn al-Wardi did not take the material for his first chapter directly from Yāqūt, the foregoing fact suggests that he may have copied it, along with other material, from al-Ḥanbali, who in turn may have taken it from Yāqūt.

[5] The same statement is found in al-Qazwīni, *ʿAjāʾib*, p. 144. It is possible that this concept may be derived from Democritus, who, according to Zeller, "imagined the earth as a round disc poised on the air and hollowed out in the middle in the form of a basin." See Eduard Zeller, *Outlines of the History of Greek Philosophy,* ed. Wilhelm Nestle, (13th ed.; London, 1950), p. 67. See also Plutarch, "Sentiments Concerning Nature," *The Complete Works of Plutarch,* (New York, 1909), III, 94.

[6] A fragment attributed to Anaximenes reads as follows: "The earth was like a table in shape." Aët. III 10, 3 (Diels, *Vors.*, 13A20). See also Kathleen Freeman, *Companion to the Pre-Socratic Philosophers,* (Oxford, 1949), p. 69.

[7] This statement is found in al-Qazwīni, *ʿAjāʾib,* p. 144. According to Leucippus, "The earth, in the centre, is shaped like a flat drum or tambourine." Aët. III 10, 4 (Diels, *Vors.* 67A26 and 27A1). This view is discussed in Freeman, *Companion,* p. 288. Aristotle refers to the same concept: "Some think it is spherical, others that it is flat and drum-shaped." Arist. *De Caelo*, Bk. II, chap. xiii, 293b35.

Some of them have alleged that it is shaped like a dome, similar to a hemisphere, and that the heaven is mounted upon its edges. [1] Others have maintained that it is elongated like a stone cylinder or pillar. [2]

One group has said that the earth stretches downward to infinity and that the heaven stretches upward to infinity. [3] Another group has asserted that what is seen of the movement of the planets is but the movement of the earth and not that of the celestial spheres. [4] Others have maintained that the various parts of the earth hold each other. [5] Some have stated that the earth is located in a void, and that there is no end to that void. [6] Aristotle has said that beyond the world there is a vacuum great enough for the heaven to breathe in. [7] Many of the ancients have alleged that the rotation of the celestial spheres over the earth holds it in the center from all sides. [8]

[1] Cf. Ibn Rustah, *B.G.A.*, VII, 23.

[2] Cf. *ibid.* Anaximander says: "The earth is like a stone column." Aët. III 10, 2 (Diels, *Vors.*, 12B5); English translation in Freeman, *Ancilla to the Pre-Socratic Philosophers*, (Oxford, 1948), p. 19, no. 5. Another source gives Anaximander's statement as follows: "He says that the earth is cylindrical in form, and that its depth is as a third of its breadth." Plut. *Strom.* 2 (Diels, *Vors.*, 12A10); English translation in John Burnet, *Early Greek Philosophy*, (London, 1920), p. 64 (no. 20). See also *ibid*, pp. 64-65.

[3] The same statement is found in Ibn Rustah, *B.G.A.*, VII, 24. This view is attributed to Xenophanes, who is reported to have said: "This is the upper limit of the earth that we see at our feet, in contact with the air; but the part beneath goes down to infinity." Achill. *Isag.* 4 p. 34, 11 Maass (Diels, *Vors.*, 21B28); English translation in Freeman, *Ancilla*, p. 23, no. 28. Both Empedocles and Aristotle took issue with this view. Aristotle, quoting Empedocles in support of his stand, said: ". . . some have been led to assert that the earth below us is infinite, saying, with Xenophanes of Colophon, that it has 'pushed its roots to infinity' —in order to save the trouble of seeking for the cause. Hence the sharp rebuke of Empedocles, in the words, 'if the deeps of the earth are endless and endless the ample ether— Such is the vain tale told by many a tongue, poured from the mouths of those who have seen but little of the whole.' " Arist. *De Caelo*, Bk. II, chap. xiii, 294a23.

[4] This statement, in an almost identical form, is found in Ibn Rustah, *B.G A.*, VII, 23-24. The same statement appears in al-Qazwīni, who attributes it to certain "followers of Pythagoras." Al-Qazwīni, *ʿAjāʾib*, p. 144. Two Pythagoreans of Syracuse, Hicetas and Ecphantus, are known to have held this view. Hicetas held that "the whole heavens with sun, moon, and stars, stand still; the earth alone moves, revolving with great rapidity on its axis, thus creating the same appearance as if the earth stood still." Cic. *Acad. Pr.* II 39, 123 (Diels, *Vors.*, 50A1); Freeman, *Companion*, p. 241. Ecphantus believed that "the earth revolves on its own axis, towards the east, and that this, not a change in its position in space, accounts for the phenomena of the skies." Hippol. *Refut.* I 15 (Diels, *Vors.*, 51A1); Aët. III 13, 3 (Diels, *Vors.*, 51A5); Freeman, *Companion*, p. 241.

[5] This seems to be a paraphrase of the view of Empedocles that the parts of the world came together. Philo, *De Provid.* II 60 p. 86 (Diels, *Vors.*, 31A49). This view is referred to and refuted by Aristotle. *De Caelo*, Bk. II, ch. xiii, 295a10.

[6] Plutarch attributes this concept to the Stoics. Plutarch, "Sentiments Concerning Nature," *The Complete Works of Plutarch*, (New York, 1909), III, 69.

[7] This is in reference to a statement by Anaximenes. It is interesting to trace this quotation from Plutarch to Aristotle to the original fragment of Anaximenes. "Aristotle [says] that the vacuum beyond the world is so great that the heaven has liberty to breathe into it . . ." Plutarch, "Sentiments Concerning Nature," *Complete Works*, III, 77-78. We are informed by Ibn an-Nadīm that Plutarch's *Opinions on Nature* was translated into Arabic by Qusṭa ibn Lūqa, whose work Yāqūt may have seen, judging by the closeness of the two versions of Anaximenes' statement. See Ibn an-Nadīm, *al-Fihrist*, I, 253. Aristotle's version of this statement is as follows: "The Pythagoreans, too, held that void exists and that it enters the heaven itself, which as it were inhales it, from the infinite air." Arist. *Physics*, 213b623. The original statement by Anaximenes reads as follows: "As our soul, being air, holds us together, so do breath and air surround the whole universe." Aët. I 3, 4 (Diels, *Vors.*, 13B2); English translation in Freeman, *Ancilla*, p. 19, no. 2. See also Burnet, *E.G.P.*, p. 75, (no. 28).

[8] This is the view of Empedocles. It is referred to and refuted by Aristotle: ". . . all

As for the Mutakallimūn, [1] they too are in disagreement. Hishām ibn al-Ḥakam [2] has held that under the earth there is a body which tends to rise and soar like fire and wind, and which prevents the earth from moving downwards. This body itself is not in need of support, for it is not one of those substances that tend to drop, but rather seeks to rise. [3] Abu al-Hudhayl [4] has alleged that God suspended the earth without props or support. [5] Others have said that the earth is compounded of two elements, one heavy and one light, and that the light element tends to move upwards, while the heavy element tends to move downwards. Each of these two elements is prevented from moving in the direction of the other, because of the equality of their pressures. [6]

The theory accepted by the majority of them is that the earth is round like a ball, placed inside the firmament like the yolk inside an egg. [7] The ether surrounds the earth and pulls it towards the firmament from all sides. People upon the earth are enveloped by this ether, which attracts the lightness in their bodies as the earth attracts the heaviness therein. For the earth is like the loadstone which attracts iron; animals and other objects that are upon the earth are like iron in this respect. [8]

Others eminent among them have said that the earth is in the center of the firmament, which is equidistant from it at every point and surrounds it like a circle described by a compass. Owing to the fact that the various parts of the

those who try to generate the heavens to explain why the earth came together at the centre . . . then seek a reason for its staying there; and some say, in the manner explained, that the reason is its size and flatness, others, with Empedocles, that the motion of the heavens, moving about it at a greater speed, prevents movement of the earth, as the water in a cup, when the cup is given a circular motion . . ." *De Caelo*, Bk. II, chap. xiii, 295a10. Al-Qazwīni cites this view, including the example of the cup that is whirled around. Al-Qazwīni, *ʿAjāʾib*, p. 145.

[1] The scholastic theologians. See article "Kalām" by D. B. Macdonald in *E. I.*

[2] Shiʿite theologian, died A.H. 199/A.D. 814-5. See article "Hishām B. al-Ḥakam" in *E. I.*

[3] Al-Ashʿari does not attribute this view to any particular person. He merely introduces it with the phrase "some have asserted." See Abu al-Ḥasan ʿAli al-Ashʿari, *Maqālāt al-Islāmīyīn*, ed. Hellmut Ritter, (Istanbul, 1930), II, 326_{4-6} and 572_{1-3}. Al-Baghdādi attributes this view to Ibn ar-Rāwandi. See Abu Manṣūr ʿAbd al-Qāhir ibn Ṭāhir al-Baghdādi, *Kitāb Uṣūl ad-Dīn*, (Istanbul, 1928), I, 62_3. Cf. al-Qazwīnī, *ʿAjāʾib*, p. 144.

[4] Muʿtazilite leader. Born A.H. 131/A.D. 748-9; died A.H. 235/A.D. 849-50. See article "Abu ʾl-Hudhail" by Carra De Vaux in *E. I.*

[5] This view is twice attributed to Abu al-Hudhayl by al-Ashʿari. See al-Ashʿari, *Maqālāt*, II, 326_{1-3} and 572_{8-9}.

[6] Al-Ashʿari refers to this view in two places. See *ibid.*, 326_{12} and 572_{4-5}. Al-Khayyāṭ asserts that Ibn ar-Rāwandi attributed it to an-Naẓẓām. See ʿAbd ar-Raḥīm ibn Muḥammad ibn ʿUthmān al-Khayyāṭ, *Kitāb al-Intiṣār*, ed. H. S. Nyberg, (Cairo, 1925), p. 39. See also al-Baghdādi, *Uṣūl ad-Dīn*, I, 62_4.

[7] This is a concept borrowed from Orphic cosmology. The egg as a symbol is often met with in Orphic theogonies. "The Orphics say that the sphere is like an egg, the vault of Heaven being shell, and the Aether the skin." Achill. *Isag.* 4 p. 33, 17 Maass (Diels, *Vors.*, 1B12); English translation in Freeman, *Ancilla*, p. 3, no. 12. Empedocles, who was noted for his mysticism and Orphic ideas, is said to have regarded the heavens as shaped like an egg. Aët. II 31, 4 (Diels, *Vors.*, 31A50). Al-Bīrūni states that this concept was known in India. He points out that similar views were attributed by the Greeks to Asclepius. See al-Bīrūni, *India*, ed. and trans. Edward Sachau, (London, 1914) I, pp. 221-223. See also Walter Scott, ed. and trans., *Hermetica*, "Asclepius III," (Oxford, 1924), Vol. III, pp. 136-138.

[8] This description closely parallels the first portion of a passage found in the following sources: Ibn Khurradādhbih, *B.G.A.*, VI, 4; al-Maqdisi, *B.G.A.*, III, 58; and Ibn al-Faqīh, *B.G.A.*, V, 4-5. Yāqūt inserts the rest of the passage later in his text. (See *infra*, p. 26). The same general ideas, in a considerably abbreviated form, are also found in Ibn Rustah, *B.G.A.*, VII, 8.

firmament attract the earth from every side, it does not incline towards any one part of the firmament, for the forces of the various parts of the firmament are equal. [1] This principle is illustrated by the loadstone, which attracts iron; likewise, it is in the nature of the firmament to attract the earth.

The best account that I have come upon in this respect, and the soundest, is that given by Muḥammad ibn Aḥmad al-Khwārizmi [al-Bīrūni], [2] who has said:

> The earth is in the center of the heavens, the center being, in reality, the lowest part thereof. The earth is round when viewed as a whole, and denticulated when viewed in part, because of the jutting mountains and sunken chasms. This fact does not preclude the sphericity of the earth when viewed in its entirety, for the masses of mountains, towering though they may be, are small in comparison with the entire earth. Do you not perceive that millet-sized projections [3] and depressions, made on [the surface of] a sphere whose diameter is a cubit or two, would not prevent the application of the principle of sphericity to it in an approximate manner?
>
> Were it not for this denticulation, water would have enveloped the earth from all sides and submerged it so that no part of it would have remained uncovered. For although water shares with earth the property of weight and the tendency to move downward, there is a difference between them in this respect, whereby water, as compared with earth, is lighter. For this reason, earth precipitates in water and the sediment settles at the bottom. As regards water, it does not sink into the earth itself, but seeps through that part of it which is loose and mixed with air. When water seeks to penetrate the earth in the form of vapor, it descends into it, causing the air to escape therefrom —a process which is similar to the falling of rain from the clouds. Because of the elevation of certain parts of the surface of the earth, water flowed into the deepest places and formed the seas. The water and earth together formed one ball, surrounded on all sides by the air.
>
> That portion of the air which came in contact with the sphere of the moon became heated by reason of the movement and the [resulting] friction of the two masses in contact. This produced the fire which surrounds the air and which diminishes in amount as it approaches the two poles because of the slowing of movement near them. [4]

This is shown in the first diagram on the opposite page.

Abu ar-Rayḥān [al-Bīrūni] has said:

> The plane of the equinoctial cuts the earth into two halves along a circle known as the equator, forming the northern and southern hemispheres. If you were to visualize a great circle passing over the poles of the equator, each of the two halves of the earth would [in turn] be divided into two halves. Thus the earth in its entirety would be divided into four quarters, two southern and two northern.

[1] This apparently represents Anaximander's view that "the earth swings free, held in its place by nothing. It stays where it is because of its equal distance from everything . . ." Burnet, *E.G.P.*, pp. 64-65 (No. 20). For the original fragment, see Hipp. Ref. I 6 (Diels, *Vors.*, 12A11).

[2] Scientist and mathematician, A.H. 362/A.D. 973—A.H. 448/A.D. 1048. See articles "al-Bīrūnī" by C. Brockelmann in *E.I.* and "al-Bīrūnī" by E. Wiedemann in *E. I. Supplement.* See also George Sarton, *Introduction to the History of Science,* (Baltimore, 1950), I, 707-709.

[3] The Arabic equivalent of the verb "to project" should be restored to *naṭaʾa* in both the German and the Egyptian editions.

[4] Al-Bīrūni, *Tafhīm,* pp. 45-46.

According to the findings of those who have studied this matter, [1] the oecumene does not extend beyond the limits of one of the two northern quarters. Consequently it has been called the inhabited quarter. It is like an elevated island surrounded by the seas. This quarter comprises all the known and traveled seas, islands, mountains, rivers, and deserts, as well as the towns

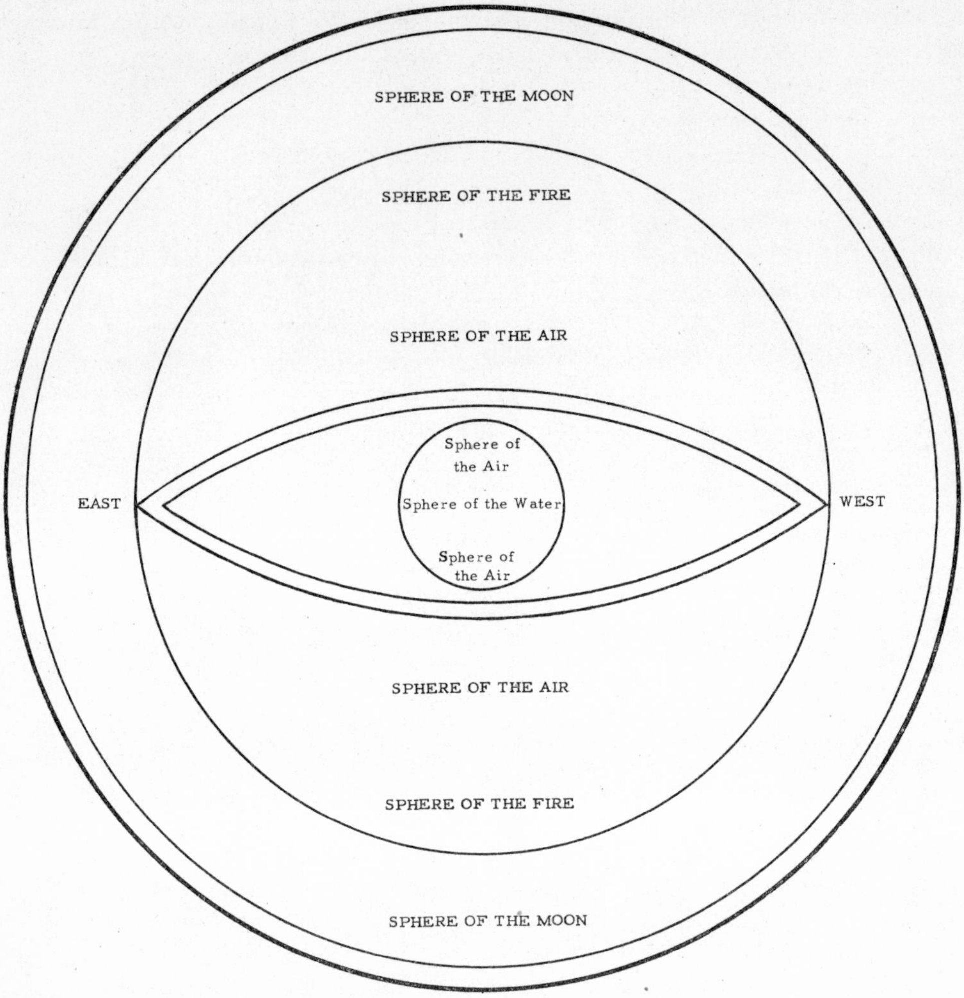

Fig. 1

and villages located therein. However, there remains a portion of this quarter, towards the north pole, which is not inhabited because of the intense cold and accumulated snows. [2]

Certain geometricians have said that, theoretically, if a hole were dug on one side of the earth it would lead to the other side. For example, if a hole were dug at Fūshanj [3] it would emerge in the land of China. They have said that people

[1] The Arabic equivalent of "those who have studied this matter" should read *al-ma'nīyūn bihā*, and not *al-mu'ayyinūn* as it appears in both the German and the Egyptian editions.

[2] This whole passage is from al-Bīrūni, *Tafhīm*, pp. 120-121. Cf. al-Qazwīni, *'Ajā'ib* p. 145, where only the first few lines are quoted.

[3] Fūshanj or Būshanj, a town in Afghanistan south of the Hāri-Rūd below Harāt. See article "Būshandj" by W. Barthold in *E. I.* Al-Bīrūni more aptly gives the example of China and Spain. See al-Bīrūni, *Tafhīm*, pp. 125-126. Cf. Shams ad-Dīn ad-Dimashqi, *Kitāb*

upon the earth are like ants upon an egg, and they have advanced numerous arguments in support of their view—some capable of being proved by demonstration, others by argument. This view is not farfetched, insofar as the earth is concerned, for that which is flat supports that which rises from it. Thus the earth is a carpet for him who is upon it, and a cover for him who is beneath it.

Writers have differed as to the area of the earth. Muḥammad ibn Mūsa al-Khwārizmi, [1] the author of the *Zīj*, has stated that the [circumference of the] earth extends 9,000 *farsakhs* in a straight line. [2] The inhabited part covers one-half of one-sixth of the earth, the remainder being devoid of habitation, plants, and animals. The seas are considered a part of the inhabited world, as are the deserts located within it.

Abu ar-Rayḥān has said that the diameter of the earth is 2,163⅔ *farsakhs* and that its circumference is 6,800 *farsakhs*. Hence its surface area amounts to 14,744,242⅕ *farsakhs*. [3]

ʿUmar ibn Jīlān [4] held that the whole world amounts to 27,000 *farsakhs*, of which the country of the Sūdān (Blacks) covers 12,000 *farsakhs*, the country of the Rūm (Byzantine empire) 8,000 *farsakhs*, the country of Fārs (Persia) 3,000 *farsakhs*, and the land of the Arabs 4,000 *farsakhs*.

Nukhbat ad-Dahr fi ʿAjāʾib al-Barr w-al-Baḥr, ed. M. A. F. Mehren, (Leipzig, 1923), pp. 9-10; Ibn al-Wardi *Kharīdat al-ʿAjāʾib*, p. 10; and al-Qazwīni, *ʿAjāʾib*, p. 146.

[1] Astronomer and mathematician of the 9th century A.D. See article "al-Khwārizmi" by E. Wiedemann in *E. I.*; Nallino, "Al-Ḫuwārizmi e il suo rifacimento della Geografia di Tolomeo," *Raccolta*, V, 458-532; and Sarton, *History of Science*, I, 563-564.

[2] According to this statement, the circumference of the earth would be 27,000 miles, and the value of a degree 75 miles. See Nallino, "Il valore metrico del grado di meridiano secondo i geografi arabi," *Raccolta*, V, 413. E. Wiedemann has taken issue with Yāqūt for attributing this statement to al-Khwārizmi. He points out: "Yāḳūt mentions (*Muʿdjam* I.16.10) Muḥammad b. Mūsa al-Khwārizmi as Ṣāḥib al-Zīdj ('author of the book of tables') apropos of a statement regarding the size of the earth; but no such statement is given in the *Zīdj*." See article "al-Khwārizmi" by E. Wiedemann in *E. I.* It should be pointed out here, however, that an identical statement attributing this measurement to al-Khwārizmi is found in Ibn al-Faqīh, whose work Yāqūt lists in his introduction as one of the primary sources of the *Muʿjam*. See Ibn al-Faqīh, *B.G.A.*, V, 3.

[3] A comparison of the figures given in al-Bīrūni's *Tafhīm* with those attributed to him by Yāqūt shows that only the figure for the circumference of the earth is the same in both texts. The diameter of the earth is given as 2,163 1/3 *farsakhs* in the *Tafhīm*, instead of 2,163 2/3 *farsakhs* as above. This discrepancy may be due to a misreading by Yāqūt or by the copyist. In giving the surface area of the earth, Yāqūt seems to have confused al-Bīrūni's figures for the area and the volume. In the *Tafhīm* these figures are given as follows:

Surface area:	14,712,720¼	square *farsakhs*
Volume:	166,744,242⅕	cubic *farsakhs*

Yāqūt evidently copied the first portion (14) of al-Bīrūni's figure for the area of the earth, but erroneously copied the last portion (744,242⅕) from al-Bīrūni's figure for the volume of the earth. See al-Bīrūni, *Tafhīm*, p. 118.

[4] It is not improbable that the above name, ʿUmar ibn Jīlān, is a composite one resulting from a combination of the names of two different persons. Al-Maqdisi attributes this statement, with a slightly different set of figures, to Abu al-Jald. De Goeje has pointed out that Abu al-Jald is the *kunyah* of the traditionist Jīlān ibn Farwah, and that Abu ʿImrān al-Jawni, among others, transmitted from him. (*B.G.A.*, IV, 62.) This fact may provide the clue needed to explain the name ʿUmar ibn Jīlān. For in Arabic, the name ʿUmar and the first three letters of the name ʿImrān, if unvocalized, read the same ,viz., "ʿmr". Furthermore, in accordance with the usual *isnād* arrangement, the name of the transmitter and his authority follow each other in close succession. These facts, coupled with the possibility that the *isnād* part of this passage may have come down in a mutilated or unintelligible condition, may account for the name ʿUmar ibn Jīlān. It should be noted that elsewhere in the text Yāqūt gives a variant of the above statement, attributing it to Qatādah (*infra*, p. 28). For other sources in which this passage occurs, see footnote no. 6, p. 28.

It has been related that according to Ardashīr [1] the earth consists of four parts. The first is the land of the Turks, which lies between the western border of India and the eastern border of the Byzantine empire. The second is the Maghrib, which lies between the western borders of the Byzantine empire and the lands of the Copts (Egyptians) and the Berbers. The third part is the land of the Sūdān, which lies between the land of the Berbers and India. The fourth part consists of those lands, attributed to the Persians, which extend from the river of Balkh (Oxus) to the limits of Adharbayjān and Persarmenia, thence to the wilderness of the Arabs, thence to ʿUmān and Makrān, and thence to Kābul and Ṭukhāristān. [2]

Dorotheus [3] has said that the earth is 25,000 *farsakhs*, of which the Turks and the Chinese have 12,000 *farsakhs*, the Byzantines, 5,000 *farsakhs*, and the Babylonians 1,000 *farsakhs*.

It has been related that Ptolemy, the author of the *Almagest*, measured Ḥarrān (Carrhae) and asserted that it is the most elevated of lands. [4] After finding its altitude to be that which he had computed, he measured a mountain of Āmid. He then went back and surveyed the distance from [5] the site of his first measurement to the site of the second on level ground, and found this distance to be 66 miles. He then multiplied it by the circle of the firmament, which is 66 degrees, and obtained 24,000 miles, which amounts to 8,000 *farsakhs*. Thereupon he alleged that the circumference of the earth encompasses 8,000 *farsakhs*. [6]

[1] This name appears incorrectly as Azdashīr in the Egyptian edition.

[2] This paragraph, attributing the division of the world to Ardashīr, is almost identical with a passage found in Ibn al-Faqīh, *B.G.A.*, V, 197. Cf. Aḥmad ibn ʿAbd al-Wahhāb an-Nuwayri, *Nihāyat al-Arab*, (Cairo, 1923), I, 207.

[3] Probably Dorotheus of Sidon, astrologer and mathematician. Ḥājji Khalīfah refers to him as Dorotheus of Alexandria, in his *Kashf aẓ-Ẓunūn*, I, 34. See also Ibn an-Nadīm, *al-Fihrist*, I, 268; Ibn al-Qifṭi, *Taʾrīkh al-Ḥukamāʾ*, p. 184; L. Schmitz, "Dorotheus," *Dictionary of Greek and Roman Biography and Mythology*, ed. William Smith, (London, 1849), I, 1068; and Kuhnert, "Dorotheos aus Sidon," in Pauly-Wissowa, *Real-Encyclopädie der Classischen Altertumswissenschaft*, V (Stuttgart, 1905), 1571.

[4] The following method of finding the circumference of the earth, which Yāqūt erroneously ascribes to Ptolemy (*circa* A.D. 150), is usually attributed to the Alexandrian geographer Eratosthenes (died *circa* 194 B.C.). See Nallino, "Il valore metrico," *Raccolta*, V, 432-433. It is the same method employed by the astronomers commissioned by the Caliph al-Maʾmūn to find the circumference of the earth in A.D. 829 and later. Eratosthenes arrived at this method by noting that at Aswān (Syene) at noon the sun was directly at the zenith, while at the same time in Alexandria, it was 7° 12' south of the zenith. From this he concluded that Alexandria was 7° 12' north of Aswān. Since he knew that the distance between the two places was 5,000 stadia, and that 7° 12' is $\frac{1}{50}$ of the full circle of 360°, he multiplied 50 by 5,000 and found the circumference of the earth to be 250,000 stadia. However, he altered the latter figure to 252,000 stadia in order to have 700 stadia to a degree. He then found the diameter of the earth to be 7, 850 miles, which figure is correct within 50 miles, according to modern measurements. See De Lacy O'Leary, *How Greek Science Passed to the Arabs*, (London, 1949), p. 30.

[5] The preposition *min* (from) appears in the German edition, but is missing in the Egyptian edition.

[6] The above figures for the value of a degree and the number of degrees in the great circle are given erroneously in both the German and the Egyptian editions. They should be restored to 66 $\frac{2}{3}$ miles and 360°, respectively. Thus 66 $\frac{2}{3}$ × 360° = 24,000 miles ÷ 3 = 8,000 *farsakhs*. Nallino, who refers to the above passage of Yāqūt's text, treats these figures as though they had been corrected, without pointing out the errors. He says: "Nella prefazione al suo gran dizionario geografico intitolato Muʿgiam al-Buldān Yāqūt scrive che Tolomeo, autore dell' Almagesto, in base a misure da lui eseguite tra Ḥarrān e i monti di Āmid, trovo per un grado di meridiano 66 $\frac{2}{3}$ miglia." In a footnote, however, reference is made to al-Masʿūdi, *al-Tanbīh w-al-Ishrāf*, *B.G.A.*, VIII, 26-27, where the correct figures are given. See Nallino, "Il valore metrico," *Raccolta*, V, 413.

A writer other than Ptolemy, [1] one to whose opinion recourse is made, has held that the earth is divided into two halves by the equator, which runs from east to west and which is the longest line on the earth-sphere, even as the ecliptic is the longest line in the firmament. The width of the earth is calculated from the south pole, around which Canopus revolves, to the north pole, around which the constellation Ursa revolves. The circumference of the earth at the equator encompasses 360 degrees, a degree being equal to 25 *farsakhs*; thus the circumference amounts to 9,000 *farsakhs* [2]. The distance from the equator to each of the two poles is 90 degrees, and its circumference widthwise is of like dimension. The inhabited part of the earth covers 24 degrees between the equator and each one [3] [of the two poles?], while the remainder of the earth is submerged by the waters of the sea. Mankind inhabits the northern quarter of the earth, while the southern quarter is desolate and the remaining half has no dweller in it. The two quarters that are visible above the [surface of the water] comprise fourteen climes. Seven of these climes are inhabited, and seven are wasteland because of the intense heat prevailing therein. Some writers have said that the inhabited region in the northern part of the earth is greater than that in the southern part. It has been said that in the northern part there are 4,000 cities. [4]

Each half of the earth consists of two quarters, the two northern quarters being [5] the half [6] that constitutes the oecumene. The northwestern quarter of the oecumene extends from [7] Iraq [westward] to al-Jazīrah, Syria, Egypt, the Byzantine empire, the land of the Franks, and Sūs (a district in southern Morocco), as well as the Fortunate Isles, which are a part thereof; the northeastern quarter extends from Iraq [eastward] to al-Ahwāz, al-Jibāl, Khurāsān and Tibet, and thence to China and Wāq Wāq. [8] Likewise, the southern half consists of two

[1] This paragraph represents the rest of the passage cut short by Yāqūt on page 21 (See footnote no. 8.) The entire paragraph, with some variations, is found in Ibn Khurradādhbih, *B.G.A.*, VI, 4. The first half of the paragraph is found in Ibn al-Faqīh, *B.G.A.*, V, 4-5, and all but the last three sentences appear in al-Maqdisi, *B.G.A.*, III, 58.

[2] According to these figures, the value of a degree would be 75 miles, and the circumference of the earth would be 27,000 miles. This passage is referred to in Nallino, "Il valore metrico," *Raccolta*, V, 417.

[3] Here Yāqūt's text seems to be corrupt, and departs from the texts of Ibn Khurradādhbih and al-Maqdisi. In both of these sources the above sentence reads as follows: "The inhabited part of the earth beyond the equator covers 24 degrees . . ."

[4] Yāqūt, unlike other sources containing this information, does not attribute it to Ptolemy. According to al-Masʿūdi, "The philosopher [Ptolemy], in his book entitled *Geography*, has given the description of the world, its cities and mountains and all that it contains of seas, islands, rivers and springs. He has described inhabited cities, and populated localities, stating that they numbered in his time 4,530 cities." (*Murūj*, I, 183-184.) Ibn Khurradādhbih, from whom Yāqūt may have obtained his information, states that Ptolemy gave the number of cities in his time as 4,200. (*B.G.A.*, VI, 5.) Commenting on this assertion of Ibn Khurradādhbih, V. V. Barthold says: "It is remarkable that even this author, who calls himself a translator of Ptolemy, attributes to Ptolemy the statement, which does not occur in the Greek original, namely, that in his times there were 4,200 towns altogether. In Ptolemy there is no such estimate of towns." See V. V. Barthold's Preface in Minorsky, *Ḥudūd*, p. 14.

[5] In both the German and Egyptian editions, the words *ar-rubʿān ash-shamālīyān* (the two northern quarters) are followed by the personal pronoun *huwa*, in the third person singular form. This pronoun should be restored to the dual form, *humā*.

[6] This word *an-niṣf* does not appear in the German edition.

[7] This preposition *min* appears in the German edition, but is missing in the Egyptian edition.

[8] There seems to be little agreement among Muslim geographers as to the identity of Wāqwāq and its location. De Goeje identifies it with Japan, but Gabriel Ferrand has taken great pains to disprove this theory. After sifting all available information, Ferrand has come

quarters: a southeastern quarter, which embraces [the lands of] the Ethiopians, the Negroes, and the Nubians; and a southwestern quarter, which has not been trodden upon by anyone on the face of the earth. [1] This quarter borders on [the land of] the Sūdān, which borders on [the land of] the Berbers, such as the Koko [2] and the like. [3]

Others have related that Ptolemy, the Greek king—who, I think, is other than the author of the *Almagest*, for the latter was not a king and did not flourish in the time of the Ptolemies but came after them—sent to this quarter a group of learned men versed in astronomy. [4] They set out to explore the land, making careful inquiries from the scientists of those countries lying near this quarter or bordering upon it. Whereupon they returned to the king and informed him that this quarter was a desolate wilderness in which there was no king, no city, and no habitation. This is called the scorched quarter; it also is called the desolate quarter.

Thereupon Ptolemy wanted to know the size of the earth and the extent of the inhabited and the desolate parts thereof. He proceeded to obtain this from the rising and the setting of the sun, which constitute a nychthemeron. He divided this [period of time] into 24 parts [i.e., equatorial hours], each equatorial hour being equal to 15 parts [i.e., time-degrees], multiplied 24 by 15, and obtained 360 parts [i.e., time-degrees]. He wanted to know the number of miles to a part [i.e., time-degree], and obtained this from the eclipse of the sun and the moon. He determined the number of hours and the number of miles from one city to another, divided the number of miles by the number of hours, and found that one part [i.e., time-degree] is equal to 75 miles. He then multiplied 75 by the 360 parts of the zodiac, and obtained 27,000 miles. Thereupon he said that the earth is round and suspended in the air, and that its circumference is 27,000 miles.

Ptolemy then examined the inhabited part of the earth [which extends] from the inhabited islands [i.e., Fortunate Isles] in the west, to the Green Sea, and thence to the farthest habitation in China. He found that if the sun rises in the aforementioned islands, it sets in China, and that if it sets in these islands, it rises in China. This encompasses one-half of the circumference of the earth, namely 13,500 miles, which is the length of the inhabited part. He also examined the inhabited part and found that it extended from the south to the north—that is, from the latitude where the day and night are equal to the latitude where in summer the day is 20 hours and the night four hours, while in winter the night is 20 hours and the day is four hours. Consequently, Ptolemy asserted that the

to the conclusion that there are two distinct Wāqwāqs: (1) the Wāqwāq of the East or the Wāqwāq of China, which he identifies with Sumatra, and (2) the Wāqwāq of Africa, which he identifies with Madagascar. See article "Wāḳwāḳ" by G. Ferrand in *E. I.*, and also his "Le Wāḳwāḳ est-il le Japon?", *Journal Asiatique* (April, 1932), pp. 193-243.

[1] The German edition has *ad-dahr* (time); the Egyptian edition has the more appropriate *al-arḍ* (earth).

[2] More properly "Gogo". This is a reference to the once flourishing town on the Niger River, southeast of Timbuktu. See Yāqūt, *Muʿjam*, IV, 172, and article "Gogo" by G. Yver in *E. I.*

[3] This paragraph, in a somewhat altered form, appears in al-Qazwīnī, *ʿAjāʾib al-Makhlūqāt*, p. 147.

[4] The following passage (ending on page 9), which deals with the results of investigations undertaken on the orders of King Ptolemy, is cited and discussed in Nallino, "Il valore metrico," *Raccolta*, V, 417-418. See also Nallino, "Storia dell' Astronomia presso gli Arabi nel Medio Evo," *ibid.*, 294-295.

day and night attain equality in an island between India and Ethiopia, to the south of the Tayman (a province of the Yaman). The inhabited world encompasses 60 parts [i.e., time-degrees], which amounts to 4,500 miles. If you were to multiply one-sixth by one-half,—which represents one-half of the circumference of the earth where night and day are equal,—you would find that the inhabited part that is known amounts to one-half of one-sixth of the earth. [1]

Others have disagreed as to the area of the earth and its size. It has been related that Makḥūl [2] has said that from the nearest to the farthest part of the earth there is a walking distance of 500 years. [3] Of these, 200 are submerged by the sea, 200 are uninhabited, 80 are inhabited by Yājūj and Mājūj [4] (Gog and Magog) and 20 are inhabited by the rest of mankind.

Qatādah [5] is reported as having said that the world amounts to 24,000 *farsakhs.* Of these, the domain of the Sūdān is 12,000 *farsakhs,* the domain of the Persians 3,000 *farsakhs,* the domain of the Byzantines 8,000 *farsakhs,* and the domain of the Arabs 1,000 *farsakhs.* [6]

According to another account, Ptolemy arrived at the approximate area and circumference of the earth in the *Almagest.* He said that the circumference of the earth is 180,000 stadia,—a stadium being equal to 400 cubits,—which amounts to 24,000 miles or 8,000 *farsakhs.* [7] This figure includes the mountains, seas, deserts, and forests therein. Ptolemy further maintained that the thickness of the earth, which is its diameter, is 7,630 miles, or 2,540 $\frac{2}{3}$ *farsakhs.* The area of the entire surface of the earth, he asserted, is 132,600,000 square miles, which amounts to 288,000 square *farsakhs.* [8]

There has been disagreement as to the nature and number of earths. God said, might and majesty be His, "It is God who has created seven heavens and as many earths."[9] It is possible that this refers to the number and layers of earths. It has been related in certain traditions that the earths have been placed one above another, and that the thickness of each earth is a walking distance of 500 years.

[1] Cf. al-Masʿūdi, *Murūj,* pp. 179-181.

[2] Abu ʿAbd Allāh ibn Abu Muslim, known as Makḥūl ash-Shāmi. A follower who died in A.H. 112 or 113. See Muḥyi ad-Dīn Abu Zakarīya Yaḥya an-Nawawi, *Kitāb Tahdhīb al-Asmā'*, ed. F. Wüstenfeld, (Göttingen, 1842), pp. 576-577.

[3] Cf. Ibn al-Wardi, *Kharīdat al-ʿAjā'ib,* pp. 10-11.

[4] The biblical Gog and Magog. Two peoples prominent in Jewish and Muslim eschatology. See article "Yādjūdj wa-Mādjūdj" by A. J. Wensinck in *E. I.*

[5] Abu al-Khaṭṭāb Qatādah ibn Diʿāmah as-Sadūsi. A Follower who died in A.H. 117 or 118. See F. Wüstenfeld, *Die Geschichtschreiber der Araber und ihre Werke,* (Göttingen, 1882), pp. 4-5.

[6] Different authors seem to have attributed this statement to different persons. Ibn al-Faqīh attributes it to Abu Khalaf. See *B.G.A.*, V, 3. Al-Maqdisi attributes it to Abu al-Jald. See *B.G.A.*, III, 62. Earlier in the text Yāqūt attributes such a statement, with slightly different figures, to ʿUmar ibn Jīlān, *supra,* p. 24. Among those who attribute it to Qatādah are: Aḥmad ibn Muḥammad ibn ʿAbd Rabbihi, *al-ʿIqd al-Farīd,* ed. A. Amīn, I. al-Abyāri, and A. S. Hārūn, (Cairo, 1949), IV, 47; and Ibn al-Wardi, *Kharīdat al-ʿAjā'ib,* p. 11.

[7] According to this measurement, the value of a degree would be 66 $\frac{2}{3}$ miles. See Nallino, "Il valore metrico," *Raccolta,* V, 413.

[8] These figures are erroneous, probably because of a corrupt text. Taking 7,630 miles as an approximately correct figure for the diameter of the earth, the surface area of the earth in square miles would be $7{,}630^2 \times \pi$, or approximately 182,894,213, instead of 132,600,000 as given in the text. In square *farsakhs,* the surface area would be $182{,}894{,}213 \div 9$, or approximately 20,321,579, and not 288,000 as above.

[9] Qur'ān LXV, 12.

Some men have attributed to each earth a people of strange appearance and characteristics, and have called each earth by a special name. [1] It has been related that ʿAṭā' ibn Yasār[2] has said concerning the words of God, might and majesty be His, "It is God who has created seven heavens and as many earths":

> In every earth there is an Adam like your Adam, and a Noah like your Noah, and an Abraham like your Abraham. [3]

But God is the most knowing.

The ancients have said that the earth comprises seven earths which border on and are adjacent to one another, and that the separation of climes follows the order of the layering and matching [of the earths]. Among the Muslims the Muʿtazilites [4] incline to this view. There are those who hold that the earth comprises seven earths [arranged] in an ascending and descending order like a staircase.

There has been disagreement concerning the seas, waters, and rivers. The Muslims have said that God created the sea bitter and salt and brought down fresh water from the heavens. For God said, may He be exalted, "And we send down water from the heavens in its due degree, and we cause it to settle on the earth . . ." [5] And all fresh water, from well or river, is from this source. When the Hour [of Judgment] draws near, God will send an angel with a basin [6] to collect these waters and return them to Paradise. The scripturaries allege that four rivers issue from Paradise: the Tigris and the Euphrates, the Sayḥūn and the Jayḥūn; [7] for they allege that Paradise is in [8] the eastern part of the world. [9]

[1] For a description of the various earths and the creatures inhabiting them, see Aḥmad ibn Muḥammad ibn Ibrāhīm ath-Thaʿlabi, *Qiṣaṣ al-Anbiyā'*, (Cairo, A.H. 1301), pp. 5-6, and Muḥammad ibn ʿAbd Allāh al-Kisā'i, *Qiṣaṣ al-Anbiyā'*, (Leyden, 1922), I, 9-10.

[2] A Follower who died *ca.* A.H. 100. See adh-Dhahabi, *Tadhkirat al-Ḥuffāẓ*, I, 84-85.

[3] According to Ibn Kathīr, this is an *athar* handed down by Ibn ʿAbbās. The version he gives is as follows: "In every earth there are people just as there are in this one. There is even an Adam like your Adam and an Abraham like your Abraham." Ibn Kathīr maintains that Ibn ʿAbbās got it from *al-Isrā'īlīyāt* (popular Jewish religious legends and beliefs current among Muslims). See Ismāʿīl ibn ʿUmar ʿImād ad-Dīn ibn Kathīr, *al-Bidāyah w-an-Nihāyah*, (Cairo, A.H. 1348), I, 21. Cf. Ibn al-Wardi, *Kharīdat al-ʿAjā'ib*, p. 10.

[4] Muslim theological school responsible for the creation of speculative dogmatics in Islam. See article "Muʿtazila" by H. S. Nyberg in *S. E. I.*

[5] Qur'ān XXIII, 18.

[6] The Arabic equivalent of the word "basin" appears as *ṭasht* in both the German and the Egyptian editions. Ibn al-Wardi, *Kharīdat al-ʿAjā'ib*, p. 11, has the more correct *ṭast*.

[7] According to Le Strange, the Arabs applied the names Jayḥūn and Sayḥūn to the Oxus and Jaxartes Rivers, later known as the Amū Daryā and Sīr Daryā. He points out that these names have also been used incorrectly to refer to the Jayḥān (Pyramus) and Sayḥān (Sarus) Rivers, which were the frontier rivers of Cilicia in the early days of Islam. Le Strange maintains that Jayḥūn and Sayḥūn are corrupt forms of the names of two rivers mentioned in Genesis, ii, 11, 13, namely Gihon and Pison. See G. Le Strange, *The Lands of the Eastern Caliphate*, (Cambridge, 1930), pp. 130-132, 434.

[8] The preposition *fi* (in) appears in the Egyptian edition, but not in the German edition.

[9] This concept is found in a number of sources, but there seems to be no general agreement as to its origin, or the names of the rivers involved. Like Yāqūt, Ibn al-Wardi mentions the above four rivers and attributes the concept to the scripturaries (*Kharīdat al-ʿAjā'ib*, pp. 11-12). Al-Qazwīni also gives these four rivers, but does not indicate the origin of the concept (*ʿAjā'ib al-Makhlūqāt*, p. 185). Al-Muṭahhar gives a somewhat different list of rivers, namely the Sayḥān, the Euphrates, and the Nile, and attributes it to the scripturaries. (al-Muṭahhar ibn Ṭāhir al-Maqdisi, *Kitāb al-Bad' w-at-Ta'rīkh*, ed. Cl. Huart, [Paris, 1907], IV, 60). Ibn al-Faqīh mentions the same rivers as al-Muṭahhar, but describes the statement as a *khabar*. Later in his book he cites the opinion of the Companion Ibn ʿAbbās to the effect that the Sayḥān is the Tigris, and the Jayḥān the River of Balkh, i.e., the Oxus. (*B.G.A.*, V, 64, 95). Al-Masʿūdi, like Ibn al-Faqīh, describes the statement as a *khabar*. However, he gives the

As regards the location of the seas in the oecumene, the best account that has reached me in this respect is the one given by Abu ar-Rayḥān al-Bīrūni, who said

The sea that lies to the west of the oecumene and along the coasts of the lands of Ṭanjah (Tangier) and al-Andalus (Spain) has been called the Encircling Sea, and the Greeks have called it Okeanos (Ocean). It is not deeply ventured into, but is navigated along its shores. The sea stretches from those lands toward the north, along the land of the Ṣaqālibah (Slavs). A great gulf issues from it north of [the land of] the Slavs, extending to the neighborhood of the land of the Muslim Bulghārs. It is known to them as the Sea of the Warank, [1] who are a nation occupying its coasts. It then turns behind them toward the east. Between its coast and the farthest limits of the land of the Turks there are lands and mountains that are unknown, desolate, and untraveled.

As for the extension of the Western Encircling Sea, from the land of Ṭanjah southwards, it swerves towards the south along the lands of the Western Sūdān, beyond the mountains known as the Mountains of the Moon, from which spring the sources of Egypt's Nile. Its navigation is fraught with peril, [2] from which no ship escapes.

As for the Encircling Sea in the east, beyond the farthest limits of the land of China, it too is untraveled. A gulf branches from it, forming the sea which has been named after every land adjacent to it, becoming first the China Sea and then the Indian Ocean. From it issue other great gulfs, each of which is separately called a sea, such as the Sea of Fārs and the Sea of Basrah, on whose eastern shores lies Tīz of Mukrān, and on whose western shores lies the port of ʿUmān.

When the sea passes beyond ʿUmān, it reaches the country of ash-Shiḥr, from which is brought frankincense and myrrh, and thence to Aden. Two large gulfs branch out from it there. One of these is known as the Sea of Qulzum [3] (Red Sea), which turns and surrounds the land of the Arabs, causing it to be like an island. Because Ethiopia is on this sea, opposite the Yaman, the sea is named after both of them, the southern part being called the Sea of Ethiopia, the northern part the Sea of the Yaman, and the two combined, the Sea of Qulzum. The reason for its being known as the Sea of Qulzum is that Qulzum, a town in the land of Syria, is at its [northern] extremity, where it narrows and where the traveler turns along its shores towards the land of the Bujah. [4]

The other gulf mentioned above is the one known as the Sea of the Berbers,

rivers of Paradise as the Nile, the Euphrates, the Tigris, and the Sayḥān, which he says is a river in Cilicia (*Murūj*, II, 358-359). According to al-Maqdisi, who gives no indication as to the source of the concept, the four rivers are the Nile, the Jayḥūn, the Euphrates, and ar-Russ, or Araxes (*B.G.A.*, III, 23). The origin of this concept may be traced to a number of *ḥadīths*, particularly to one transmitted on the authority of Abu Hurayrah which is reported in the *Musnad* of Ibn Ḥanbal and the *Ṣaḥīḥ* of Muslim. According to Ibn Ḥanbal's version of this *ḥadith*: "Four rivers gush forth from Paradise: the Euphrates, the Nile, the Sayḥān, and the Jayḥān" (*Musnad*, II, 260-261). As-Suyūṭi examines this *ḥadīth* critically and, after citing other *ḥadīths* in its support, concludes that it is a genuine one (*al-La'āli'*, I, 94). Ibn Kathīr, who cites both versions of this *ḥadīth*, identifies "the Sayḥūn or the Sayḥān" and "the Jayḥūn or the Jayḥān" as two rivers of Cilicia (*al-Bidāyah w-an-Nihāyah*, I, 26 and 28).

[1] The Sea of the Varangians, or the Baltic. V. Minorsky cites this passage and refers to the confusion between the Baltic and Azov Seas found in certain medieval sources. See Minorsky, *Ḥudūd*, pp. 180-182.

[2] The word *gharar* (peril), which is erroneously transcribed as *ghazr* in both the German and the Egyptian editions, is corrected in the former ("Anmerkungen," *Muʿjam*, V, 2).

[3] The Greek Clysma. See article "al-Ḳulzum" by E. Honigmann in *E.I.*

[4] The Beja, a group of Hamitic tribes living in the northern Sudan between the Nile and the Red Sea. See article "Bedja" by C. H. Becker in *E.I.*, and A. Paul, *A History of the Beja Tribes* (Cambridge, England, 1954).

which stretches from Aden to Sufālah[1] of the Zanj, beyond which no ship ventures because of the great risks involved. Beyond this point it joins the Western Ocean. In the eastern part of this sea are the islands of the Zābaj,[2] the islands of the Dībajāt,[3] then Qumayr,[4] and then the islands of the Zanj. One of the greatest of these islands is the island known as Sarandīb (Ceylon), which is called Sankadīb[5] in the language of India. From it are brought all

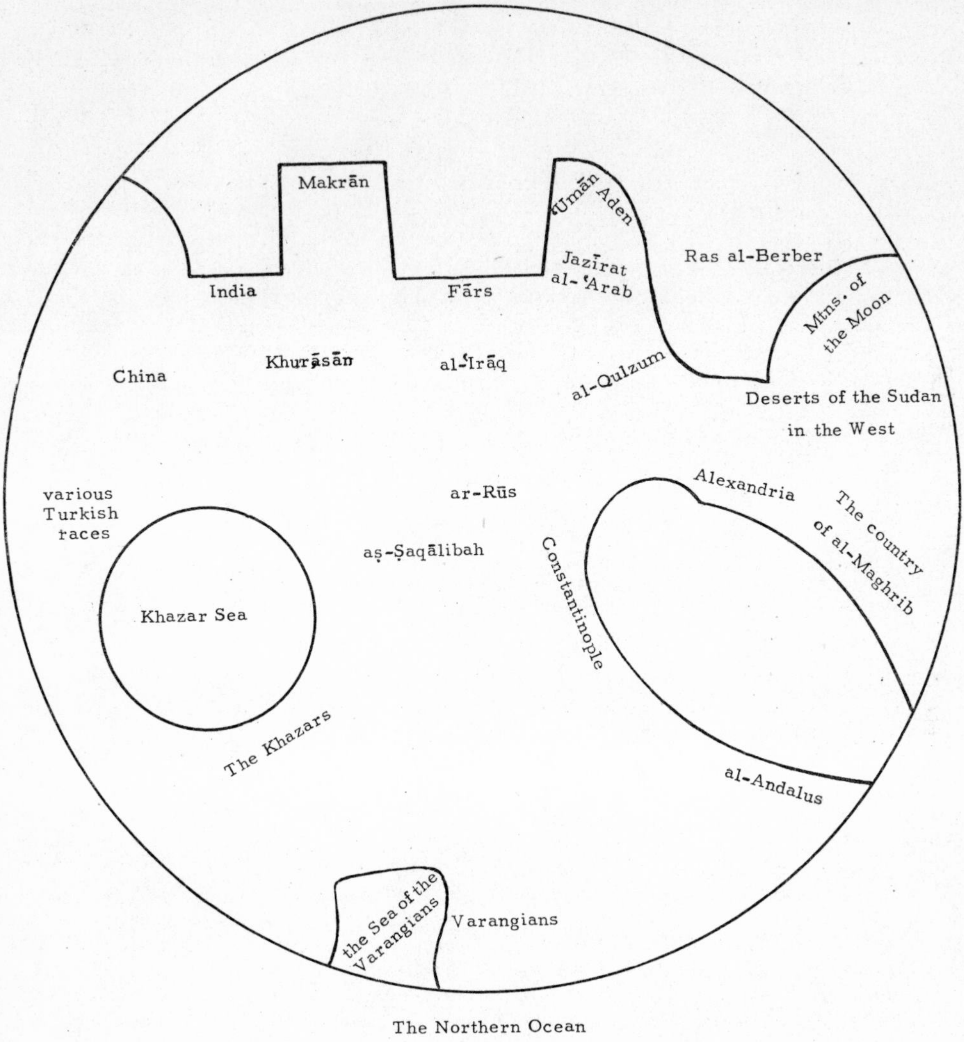

Fig. 2.

[1] A district and town of East Africa, in the southern part of Portuguese Mozambique. See article "Sofāla" by G. Ferrand in *E.I.*, and Minorsky, *Ḥudūd*, p. 472.

[2] More correctly "Zābag." According to Ferrand, it is to be identified with Sumatra. See article "Zābag" by G. Ferrand in *E.I.*

[3] The Laccadives and Maldives. Ferrand explains the name as follows: Dībajāt = dība < Skr. dvīpa, island + the Persian plural suffix, *-jāt*. See Gabriel Ferrand, *Relations de voyages et textes géographiques arabes, persans et turks relatifs à l'Extrême-Orient,* (Paris, 1913) I, 35, 202.

[4] Apparently the Arabic version of Khmer. See *ibid.*, 202.

[5] According to Ferrand, this name should be read Sinkadīb < Skr. Simhadvīpa, the Island of the Lion. *Ibid.*

kinds of corundum and tin (*ar-raṣāṣ al-qalʿi*).[1] Camphor is brought from Surbizah.[2]

In the center of the oecumene, in the land of the Slavs and the Rūs, there is a sea known to the Greeks as Pontus (Black Sea), and known to us as the Sea of Ṭarābuzindah (Trebizond), which is a port on it. From this sea issues a gulf that skirts the walls of the city of Constantinople and continues to narrow until it joins the Sea of Syria [i.e., the Mediterranean], on whose southern shores lie the countries of the Maghrib, stretching as far as Alexandria and Egypt. Opposite them, to the north, lie the lands of al-Andalus (Spain) and the Byzantine empire. This sea flows into the Encircling Sea near Spain, through the straits mentioned in books as the Crossing of Hercules and now known as az-Zuqāq.[3]

Near Ṭabaristān is the sea of the port of Jurjān. On it lies the town of Ābaskūn,[4] by whose name the sea is known. From there it extends to Ṭabaristān and the land of the Daylam, to Shirwān and Bāb al-Abwāb (Derbent), then to the territory of al-Lān (the Alans), then to the land of the Khazars, then to the river Itil (Volga), then to the habitations of the Ghuzzīyah[5] (Ghuzz Turks), and finally back to Ābaskūn again. This sea has been named after every land adjacent to it. Among us, however, it has been known as the Sea of the Khazars; among the ancients, as the Sea of Jurjān. Ptolemy called it the Sea of Arqaniyah (Hyrcania). This sea is not connected with any other sea.

As for the rest of the waters gathered in the various places of the earth, they consist of swamps and marshes. These waters may, perhaps, be called lakes, such as Lake Afāmiyah (Apamea), Lake Ṭabarīyah (Tiberias), and Zughar (Dead Sea) in the land of Syria; and Lake Khwārizm (Aral Sea) and Lake Issik-Kul[6] near[7] Barsakhān.[8]

The approximate figure of what we have discussed may be seen within the circle in the second diagram on the opposite page [here on p. 31].

There has been disagreement as to the reason for the saltness of sea water. Some have maintained that because it stood for a long time and the sun persisted in scorching it, sea water became bitter and salt.[9] Because the air attracted

[1] See article "Ḳalʿī" by M. Streck in *E. I.*

[2] More properly Sribuzah. See Ferrand, *Relations de voyages*, I, 202.

[3] Literally, "the lane." See article "Gibraltar" by C. F. Seybold in *E. I.*, where, among other things, this Arabic name for the famous straits is cited.

[4] A town located on the southeastern shore of the Caspian Sea. It was one of the most important Caspian ports in the Middle Ages, until it was submerged by the rising level of that sea when the Oxus temporarily flowed into it as the result of a change in its course. See article "Ābaskūn" by M. Streck in *E. I.*, article "Abaskūn" by V. Minorsky in *E. I.* (new edition), and Minorsky, *Ḥudūd*, p. 386, note 5. For the various names by which the Caspian Sea was known to Arab geographers, see article "Baḥr al-Khazar" (unsigned) in *E. I.*

[5] The Arabic name for the Oghuz branch of the Turkish people. See article "Ghuzz" by W. Barthold in *E. I.*

[6] In the text, Issik-Kul is erroneously transcribed as Ābaskūn, due to an error by the copyist. Cf. al-Bīrūni, *Tafhīm*, p. 124, where this name appears correctly as Issik-Kul. Barthold observes the same error in Yāqūt's text, ". . . where some copyist substituted for the name of Issik-Kul that of the port of Abaskūn on the Caspian." However, due to a typographical error, Barthold's reference is given as "Yāqūt, II, 22_4" instead of I, 22_4. See "V. V. Barthold's Preface," Minorsky, *Ḥudūd*, p. 28.

[7] Owing to a typographical error, the word *bil-qurb* (near) is misspelled *bil-qura* in the Egyptian edition.

[8] Compare the Arabic text of al-Bīrūni, *Tafhīm*, pp. 121-124. Except for minor discrepancies, the above passage is identical in the two texts.

[9] This quotation is from Anaximander, who said: "The sea is what is left of the original moisture, the fire has dried up most of it and turned the rest salt by scorching it." Aët. III 16, 1 (Diels, *Vors.*, 12A27); for English translation, see Burnet, *E.G.P.*, p. 64 (no. 20.)

its lighter parts, [1] sea water is what remains of the moisture strained by the earth. [2] This accounts for its heaviness. Others have held that in the sea there are roots which change sea water, and that as a result, it has become bitter and salt. [3] Still others have declared that water is one of those substances subject to change through admixture; hence, the taste of every body of water acquires the taste of its soil. [4]

There has been disagreement concerning the mountains. God Most High has said: "And He set in the earth firm mountains lest it should move with you . . ." [5] He also said, "Have we not made the earth like unto an expanse, and the mountains like unto stakes?" [6] It has been related that a certain Greek said that in the beginning the earth rocked because of its small size, but with the passage of time it solidified and became stable. [7] This view is confirmed by the Qur'ān. The Qur'ān, however, adds that the earth has been made stable by the mountains. There are those who have held that the mountains are the bones of the earth, and its roots.

There has been disagreement concerning that which is under the earth. Some of the ancients have alleged that the earth is surrounded by water, and the water is surrounded by air, and the air is surrounded by fire, and the fire is surrounded by the lowest heaven, which in turn is surrounded by the second heaven, then the third, and so on, to the seventh [heaven], and the latter is surrounded by the sphere of the fixed stars. Above the sphere of the fixed stars is the equinoctial, above the equinoctial is the world of the soul, above the world of the soul is the world of the mind, and above the world of the mind is the Creator, exalted be His greatness. Beyond Him there is nothing. According to this arrangement, the sky is below the earth, as it is above it. [8]

[1] "The drinkable, sweet water, then, is light and is all of it drawn up: the salt water is heavy and remains behind . . ." Aristot., *Meteorologica*, 355a34 and 355b4-9. Alexander of Aphrodisias, in his commentary on Aristotle's *Meteorologica*, attributes this statement to Diogenes of Apollonia. According to Freeman, *Companion*, p. 281, Diogenes maintained that "the sea is salt because the sun draws up the sweet, that is, the fresh water, and the residue is salty." Alex. *Meteor.* B 1 (353a32) p. 67 (Diels, *Vors.*, 64A17).

[2] A number of Greek philosophers have speculated about this matter. According to Freeman, *Companion*, p. 329, Metrodorus of Chios said that "the sea is salt because it trickles through the earth and takes to itself part of the solid substance through which it passes, like something percolating through ashes." Alex. *Meteor.* p. 67, 17. Aët. III 16, 6 (Diels, *Vors.*, 70A19). As Freeman points out, Anaxagoras also believed that "the saltness of the sea was explained by the percolation of water through the earth, which contains salt . . ." See Freeman, *Companion*, p. 271. For the original fragment, see Diels, *Vors.*, 59A90.

[3] According to Aristotle, "The old writers who invented theogonies say that the sea has springs, for they want earth and sea to have foundations and roots of their own." Aristot. *Meteorologica*, 353a31.

[4] Aristotle has commented on the above as follows: "Again, if it is maintained that an admixture of the earth makes the sea salt (for they say that the earth has many flavors and is washed down by the rivers and so makes the sea salt by its admixture), it is strange that rivers should not be salt too." *Ibid.*, 357a14.

[5] Qur'ān XVI, 15.

[6] Qur'ān LXXVIII, 6-7.

[7] This apparently refers to a statement attributed to Democritus. According to Freeman, *Companion*, p. 305, Democritus maintained that "the earth was originally in motion, while still small and light; but as it grew heavier and heavier by the accumulation of more material, it finally came to rest." Aët. III 13, 4 (Diels, *Vors.*, 68A95).

[8] The first part of this statement is obviously based on the Empedoclean doctrine of the four elements,—fire, air, water, and earth. Empedocles imagined that above the realm of matter there existed a realm of the blessed spirits. See Zeller, *Outlines*, pp. 56, 58-59, and

In the narratives of Muslim storytellers there are strange things which wise men find difficult to accept. Some of these tales I relate without believing in their veracity. They have related that God the Most High created the earth tossing as a ship tosses. [1] Thereupon God sent an angel, who entered under the earth and placed the rock upon his shoulders. The angel thrust out his hands, one to the east and the other to the west, grasped the seven earths and controlled them, and they were calm. But there was no resting place for the feet [of the angel]. Thereupon God caused a bull, with 40,000 horns and 40,000 limbs, [2] to be sent down from Paradise, in order that the feet of the angel might rest upon its hump. But the feet of the angel did not reach the hump, so God sent a green corundum from Paradise, its dimensions being a walking distance of so many thousands of years. He placed it upon the hump of the bull, and the feet of the angel came to rest upon it.

The horns of the bull pass through the [four] quarters of the earth, and they are entwined under the Throne [of God]. The nostrils of the bull are placed against two holes in the rock which is under the sea, and every day it breathes two breaths. When the bull breathes in, the sea ebbs and when it breathes out, the sea flows.

But there was no resting place for the limbs of the bull, so God, may He be exalted, created a sand-dune (*kathīb*) [3] as thick as the seven heavens and the seven earths. And the limbs of the bull came to rest upon it. But there was no resting place for the sand-dune, so God, may He be exalted, created a whale named Balhūt. [4] He placed the sand-dune on the dorsal fin of the whale, the dorsal fin being the wing which is in the middle of the back of a fish. The whale, which is on the back of the sterile wind, is held in check by a chain, as thick as the [seven] heavens and the [seven] earths, which is fastened to the Throne.

It is said that Iblīs (the Devil) went to the whale and told him, "God has not created a creature greater than you. Why, then, do you not cause the world to quake?" As the whale was about to do something of the sort, God subjected him to a gnat which plagued his eyes and distracted him. Others have alleged that God subjected him to a sword-like [5] fish and that he is awed by it and occupied in watching it.

Burnet, *E.G.P.*, p. 236. The cosmic system described above by Yāqūt is apparently a Muslim version. For a comparison with other cosmic systems current among the Greeks, including those of Philolaus, Parmenides, and the Neo-Platonists, see C. J. De Vogel, *Greek Philosophy: A Collection of Texts*, (Leyden, 1950), I, 19-20, 41, 42.

[1] The two earliest sources in which the following cosmological story appears are ath-Thaʿlabi, *Qiṣaṣ al-Anbiyāʾ*, and al-Kisāʾi, *Qiṣaṣ al-Anbiyāʾ*. It is very probable that Yāqūt used both sources. Notwithstanding a few points to the contrary, Yāqūt's version is much closer to that of ath-Thaʿlabi. cf. al-Qazwīni, *ʿAjāʾib*, p. 145.

[2] This figure is given in ath-Thaʿlabi's text as 70,000, whereas al-Kisāʾi, like Yāqūt, gives 40,000. Al-Kisāʾi, however, also endows the bull with 40,000 eyes, ears, mouths and tongues.

[3] In Yāqūt's text this appears as "kumkum", an obscure word whose meaning it has not been possible to ascertain. The editor of an-Nuwayri's *Nihāyat al-Arab*, where the story of the world-supporting bull appears in an abbreviated form (p. 91), has this comment by way of an explanation in the footnote: "sic!". In Ibn al-Wardi it appears as *kathīb* (sand-dune), which word has been adopted in this translation in place of *kumkum*.

[4] Cf. Ibn al-Wardi, *Kharīdat al-ʿAjāʾib*, p. 14, where this word appears as *bahmūt*, apparently a loan-word from the Hebrew *behēmōth*.

[5] In the German edition, *k-ash-shabṭah*; in the Egyptian edition more correctly *k-ash-shaṭbah* (sword-like).

It has been said that God, may He be exalted, caused the mountain Qāf [1] to grow out of the corundum that is upon the hump of the bull, and it surrounded the earth. Thus the mountain Qāf originated from a green corundum, and it has been said that the greenness of the sky is therefrom. But God is the most knowing. Furthermore, it has been said that between the mountain Qāf and the heaven is the figure of a man who has a head and a face and a tongue. Then God the Most High caused mountains to grow out of Qāf, and made them to be as stakes to the earth, even as roots are to the trees. [2]

When God, might and majesty to Him, wishes to cause a town to quake, He commands the angel, "Let such a town quake." Whereupon the angel moves the root which is under that town, and causes it to quake. When God wishes a town to be swallowed up, He commands the angel, "Overturn the root that is under it." Whereupon the angel overturns it, and the town is swallowed up.

Wahb ibn Munabbih [3] has alleged that the bull and the whale swallow that which is drained of the waters of the earth. When their bellies are filled, the Day of Judgment will be at hand.

Others have said that the earth is upon the water, and the water is upon the rock, and the rock is upon the hump of the bull, and the bull is upon a dense sand-dune, and the sand-dune is upon the back of the whale, and the whale is upon the sterile wind, and the wind is upon a veil of darkness, and the darkness is upon the humid soil. Here ends the knowledge of human beings, and no one save God knows what is beyond that. God said, may He be exalted, "His, whatsoever is in the heavens and whatsoever is in the earth, and whatsoever is between them both, and whatsoever is beneath the humid soil." [4]

The author of this book, ʿUbayd Allāh [Yāqūt], who is in need of God, declares that we have related but little of much that has been said in this respect. There is no limit to the confusion and controversy concerning these matters, save that which we have set by confining ourselves to what we have related. Hardly does he who has learning set store by them or he who is wise rely upon them. For these are but tales that storytellers have told with the object of awing the common people. These tales were composed in a manner commensurate with the mentality of the common people and have no basis in reason or traditional knowledge.

In all this, there is nothing that can be relied upon save a tradition related by Abu Hurayrah [5] from the Prophet. It is the one that we have had the pleasure of hearing from Ḥanbal ibn ʿAbd Allāh ibn al-Faraj ibn Saʿādah Abu ʿAli al-Mukabbir al-Baghdādi, [6] who said:

[1] In Muslim cosmology, Qāf is the mountain range which encircles the world. According to popular belief, all mountains branch out from it and are connected with it by subterranean branches and veins. If God wishes to destroy any region, He simply orders one of these branches to be set in motion. The main features of the Muslim idea of the mountain of Qāf seem to have been borrowed from the Persians. For further details, see article "Ḳāf" by M. Streck in *E. I.*

[2] The same concept is found in ath-Thaʿlabi, *Qiṣaṣ al-Anbiyāʾ*, p. 4; al-Kisāʾi, *Qiṣaṣ al-Anbiyāʾ*, p. 9; and Niʿmat Allāh al-Jazāʾiri, *an-Nūr al-Mubīn fi Qiṣaṣ al-Anbiyāʾ w-al-Mursalīn*, (Najaf, Iraq, A.H. 1355), p. 112.

[3] Early Muslim writer familiar with Jewish and Christian literature, A.H. 34—A.H. 110 or 114. See article "Wahb ibn Munabbih" by J. Horovitz in *E. I.*

[4] Qur'ān XX, 5.

[5] A Companion of the Prophet and one of the most zealous transmitters of *ḥadīth*. See article "Abu Huraira" by I. Goldziher in *E. I.*

[6] Abu ʿAli Ḥanbal ibn ʿAbd Allāh ibn al-Faraj al-Baghdādi ar-Ruṣāfi al-Mukabbir. A Ḥanbali traditionist, died A.H. 604. See adh-Dhahabi, *Mīzān al-Iʿtidāl fi Naqd al-Rijāl*,

We were informed by Abu al-Qāsim Hibat Allāh ibn al-Ḥuṣayn, [1] who said, It was told us by Abu ʿAli ibn Muḥammad ibn al-Mudhahhib, [2] who said, It was told us by Abu Bakr Aḥmad ibn Jaʿfar ibn Ḥamdān ibn Mālik al-Qaṭīʿi [3] in the form of a reading delivered in his presence (*qirāʾatan ʿalayhi*) in the year A.H. 366. He said, It was told us by Abu ʿAbd ar-Raḥmān ʿAbd Allāh ibn Aḥmad ibn Muḥammad ibn Ḥanbal, [4] who said, It was told us by my father, [5] who said, It was told us by Shurayḥ, [6] who said, It was told us by al-Ḥakam ibn ʿAbd al-Mālik, [7] who had it from Qatādah, who had it from al-Ḥasan [al-Baṣri] [8] who had it from Abu Hurayrah, who said:

While we were at [the home of] the Apostle of God, a cloud passed, and he said, 'Do you know what that is which is above you?' We said, 'God and His Apostle are the most knowing.' He said, 'This is a rain cloud which floods the earth, and which God directs to those among His servants who do not give thanks to Him, and who do not call Him Lord.'

He then said, 'Do you know what that is which is above you?' We said, 'God and His Apostle are the most knowing.' He said, 'The first heaven (ar-Raqīʿ), which is a covered wave and a preserved ceiling. Do you know how much there is between you and it?' We said, 'God and His Apostle are the most knowing.' He said, 'A walking distance of 500 years.'

He then said, 'Do you know what is above it?' We said, 'God and His Apostle are the most knowing.' He said, 'Another heaven. Do you know how much there is between you and it?' We said, 'God and His Apostle are the most knowing.' He said, 'A walking distance of 500 years.' He went on in this manner until he had enumerated seven heavens.

He then said, 'Do you know what is beneath you?' We said, 'God and His Apostle are the most knowing.' He said, 'The earth. Do you know what is beneath it?' We said, 'God and His Apostle are the most knowing.' He said, 'Another earth. Do you know how much there is between you and it?' We said, 'God and His Apostle are the most knowing.' He said, 'A walking distance of 700 years.' He went on in this manner until he had enumerated seven earths.

He then said, 'By God, if you were to lower one of you by a rope to the seventh and the lowermost earth, it would take you unto God.' He then recited, 'He is the First and the Last, the Seen and the Hidden, and He knoweth all things!' [9]

(Cairo, A.H. 1325), I, 291. Abu al-Maḥāsin al-Ḥusayni ad-Dimashqi, *Dhayl Tadhkirat al-Ḥuffāẓ*, (Damascus, A.H. 1347) p. 33, note 1.

[1] Traditionist, died A.H. 525. See ʿAbd al-Ḥayy ibn al-ʿImād al-Ḥanbali, *Shadharāt adh-Dhahab fi Akhbār man Dhahab*, (Cairo, A.H. 1350), IV, 77; Abu al-Maḥāsin, *Dhayl Tadhkirat al-Ḥuffāẓ*, p. 33, note 2.

[2] Traditionist, A.H. 355—444. See adh-Dhahabi, *Mīzān al-Iʿtidāl*, I, 237; Abu al-Maḥāsin, *Dhayl Tadhkirat al-Ḥuffāẓ*, p. 33, note 3.

[3] Traditionist, died A.H. 367. See *ibid.* p. 33, note 4; adh-Dhahabi, *Mīzān*, p. 41; and Abu al-Ḥusayn Muḥammad ibn Abi Yaʿla, *Ṭabaqāt al-Ḥanābilah*, ed. Muḥammad Ḥāmid al-Faqi, (Cairo, 1952), II, 6.

[4] Son of Aḥmad ibn Ḥanbal. He compiled the great collection of traditions known as the *Musnad* from lectures delivered by his father. See *ibid.*, I, 180-188.

[5] Founder of the Ḥanbali school and father of the foregoing. A.H. 164/A.D. 780—A.H. 241/A.D. 855. See article "Aḥmad ibn Muḥammad ibn Ḥanbal" by I. Goldziher in *E. I.*

[6] Abu Umayyah Shurayḥ ibn al-Ḥarath ibn Qays, a leading Follower and judge of al-Kūfah. Died circa A.H. 80, aged 100, according to some reports, and 120, according to others. See Abu al-ʿAbbās Aḥmad ibn Khallikān, *Wafayāt al-Aʿyān*, ed. and trans. M. De Slane, (Paris, 1843-7), I, 316-317.

[7] Traditionist. See Ibn Ḥajar al-ʿAsqalāni, *Kitāb Tahdhīb at-Tahdhīb*, (Ḥaydarābād, A.H. 1325), II, 431-432, and adh-Dhahabi, *Mīzān al-Iʿtidāl*, I, 270.

[8] Outstanding theologian and *ḥadīth* transmitter. A.H. 21/A.D. 642- A.H. 110/A.D. 728. See article "al-Ḥasan" (unsigned) in *E. I.*

[9] Qurʾān LVII, 3.

I say that this is a sound *ḥadīth*, [1] traced by Abu ʿĪsa Muḥammad ibn ʿĪsa ibn Sawrah at-Tirmidhi, [2] from ʿAbd ibn Humayd, [3] from Yūnus, [4] from Shaybān ibn ʿAbd ar-Raḥmān, [5] from Qatādah, from al-Ḥasan al-Baṣri, from Abu Hurayrah.

The wording of the tradition varies, but the meaning is the same.

[1] The text of the above *ḥadīth* is found in Ibn Ḥanbal, *Musnad*, II, 370. For another very similar version, see at-Tirmidhi, *Ṣaḥīḥ*, with commentary by Ibn al-ʿArabi, (Cairo, 1931-34), XII, 182-183. According to Wensinck, *C.T.M.*, II, 291, the *ḥadīth* compilations of Ibn Ḥanbal and at-Tirmidhi are the only ones that contain this *ḥadīth*. It will be seen from the above that while Yāqūt used Ibn Ḥanbal's version in his text, he turned to at-Tirmidhi for further verification.

[2] Compiler of one of the six canonical collections of *ḥadīth* known after his name. Died A.H. 279/A.D. 892. See article "al-Tirmidhi" by A. J. Wensinck in *E. I.*

[3] ʿAbd ibn Ḥumayd ibn Naṣr. Traditionist, died A.H. 249. See adh-Dhahabi, *Tadhkirat al-Ḥuffāẓ*, II, 104.

[4] Yūnus ibn Muḥammad al-Muʾaddib. Traditionist, died A.H. 280. See Ibn Saʿd, *Kitāb aṭ-Ṭabaqāt*, VII, Part II, 79.

[5] Grammarian and traditionist, died A.H. 164. See *ibid.*, VI, 263.

CHAPTER TWO

ON THE SEVEN CLIMES, THE DISAGREEMENT CONCERNING THEIR NATURE, AND THE ETYMOLOGY OF THE WORD *IQLĪM*

We proceed first by giving a general account of the views of the scientists in order to support and elucidate that which we shall present henceforth. It is the most forceful and succinct account that I have heard in this respect.

They said that the total surface area of the earth-sphere, by the accepted measurement, is 100,600,000 square miles, each mile being 4,000 cubits, each cubit being 24 fingers—every three miles being equal to a *farsakh*. Three-quarters of the earth's area, which comprises its entire spherical surface, is submerged by water, while the remaining quarter is unsubmerged.

The oecumene (*al-maʿmūrah*) is the inhabited part of this quarter, one-third and one-third of a tenth of which is unsubmerged, the remainder being wasteland. This portion of the inhabited quarter has an area of 33,150,000 square miles. [1] The oecumene, which lies between the equator and the north pole, is divided into seven *iqlīms* [2] (climes). There has been disagreement concerning their nature, as we shall point out presently.

Some persons have disagreed as to whether the seven climes are in both the northern and the southern hemispheres, or in the northern but not in the southern hemisphere. Hermes [3] maintained that there are seven climes in the south, as there are in the north. Others have said that this cannot be relied upon, for lack of proof.

The majority have maintained that the seven climes are in the north but not in the south, due to the abundance of habitation in the north and its sparseness in the south. Therefore they have divided the oecumene [into climes] in the north, but not in the south.

[1] There seems to be some discrepancy between the above figures. The area of the oecumene, which is said to amount to one-third and one-third of a tenth of one quarter, cannot be 33,150,000 sq. miles if the area of the entire earth, which constitutes all four quarters, amounts to 100,600,000 sq. miles.

[2] The Arabic word *iqlīm* is the arabicized form of the Greek word *klima* (inclination). Likewise the Arab concept of the climes goes back to the ancient Greeks. Eratosthenes divided the world into seven longitudinal zones, the limits of which were arbitrarily fixed, while Hipparchus made the zones equal in latitude. See article "Iḳlīm" by T. H. Weir in *E. I.*, and E. Honigmann, *Die Sieben Klimata*, (Heidelberg, 1929), pp. 10-30.

[3] Hermes Trismegistes or The Thrice Greatest Hermes. A legendary figure credited with great wisdom and knowledge. Various writings attributed to him show a curious mixture of gnostic and neo-Platonic ideas. He has sometimes been identified with the Prophet Idrīs mentioned in the Qur'ān. See Ibn al-Qifṭi, *Taʾrīkh al-Ḥukamāʾ*, pp. 1-7 and 347-350; Pauly-Wissowa, *Real-Encyclopädie*, (Stuttgart, 1913), VIII, 792-823; Walter Scott, ed. *Hermetica*, (Oxford, 1924), IV Vols.; M. Plessner, "Hermes Trismegistus and Arab Science," *Studia Islamica*, ed. R. Brunschvig and J. Schacht, (Paris, 1954), II, 45-59.

As rēgards the etymology of the term *aqālīm* (climes), they have maintained that it is an Arabic word, the singular form of which is *iqlīm*, the plural *aqālīm*. This is similar to the word *ikhrīṭ*, a kind of plant, whose plural is *akhārīṭ*. It is as though the *iqlīm* were so called because it is sliced off (*maqlūm*), that is to say cut, from the land which borders upon it. For *qalm* means cutting. From it comes [the expression] "*Qalamtu ẓufri*" (I pared my nail). *Qalam* (pen) was named after it, because it is *maqlūm*, that is to say cut, time and again. For whenever you cut something little by little, you have pared it (*qalamtahu*).

Muḥammad ibn Aḥmad Abu ar-Rayḥān al-Bīrūni has said:

> The *iqlīm*, according to Abu al-Faḍl al-Harawi,[1] in his book *al-Madkhal as-Ṣāḥibi*, is the inclination (*mayl*). It is as though by it were meant the mansions that incline away from the meridian.

He also said:

> But according to Ḥamzah ibn al-Ḥasan al-Iṣbahāni,[2] who is one skilled in the language and devoted to the study thereof, the *iqlīm* is the *rustāq* in the language of the Jarāmiqah,[3] who inhabit Syria and al-Jazīrah. They divide a kingdom into *iqlīms*, as the people of the Yaman divide a kingdom into *mikhlāfs*, and others into *kūrahs*[4] and *ṭussūjs*, and so on.

Abu ar-Rayḥān continued:

> According to Abu Ḥātim ar-Rāzi,[5] in his book *Kitāb az-Zīnah* (*The Book of Ornamentation*), *iqlīm* is the same as share (*naṣīb*). It is derived from *qalam* and is of the measure *if'īl*. For the division of shares was carried out by means of casting lots with reeds (*aqlām*) upon which were written the names of the various shares. Thus God, may He be exalted, has said, '. . . when they cast lots with their reeds, which of them should rear Mary . . .'[6]

Ḥamzah al-Iṣbahāni has said:

> The earth is spherical in shape. The inhabited portion amounts to less than one quarter of it. This quarter has been divided into two parts: the land and the sea. It has also been divided into seven parts, each of which is called *kushkhar* in the language of the Persians. The Arabs have borrowed the word *iqlīm* from the Syriac-speaking people as a name for the *kushkhar*[7]; the term *iqlīm* is a name for the *rustāq*.

[1] Aḥmad ibn Abi Sa'īd. A geometrician of the 10th century, known for his revision of the *Spherics* of Menelaos. See Ḥājji Khalīfah, *Kashf aẓ-Ẓunūn*, I, 143 and II, 2046; *G.A.L. Supplement*, I, 854; Sarton, *History of Science*, I, 254.

[2] Historian and man of letters, A.H. 280/A.D. 893-A.H. 360/A.D. 970. See *G.A.L.*, I, 145 and *G.A.L. Supplement*, I, 221.

[3] A Syriac-speaking people of Syria and Northern Mesopotamia, sometimes confused with the Jarājimah, another Syriac-speaking people. Ibn al-Faqīh, (*B.G.A.*, V, 35-36) maintains that the Jarāmiqah are the peasants (*'ulūj*) of al-Jazīrah, while the Jarājimah are the peasants of Syria. Under the entry "Jarāmiqah" in *Tāj al-'Arūs*, az-Zabīdi describes the Jarāmiqah as a non-Arab people who lived in Mosul in the early days of Islam. But he quotes al-Layth, who states that the Jarāmiqah are the Nabaṭ of Syria. In the same source under entry "Jarājimah," the latter are described as a non-Arab people of al-Jazīrah, or simply as Nabaṭ. Cf. article "Djarādjimah" (unsigned) in *E.I.*

[4] In the Egyptian edition (M.I.) this word is erroneously transcribed as "*kawthar*"; it appears correctly as *kūrah* in the Egyptian and German editions.

[5] Muḥammad ibn Idrīs ibn al-Mundhir ibn Dāwūd ibn Mihrān. Traditionist and jurist, died A.H. 273/A.D. 887. Ibn an-Nadīm, (*al-Fihrist*, I, 189) describes his *Kitāb az-Zīnah* as a large book which treats of jurisprudence and similar subjects. See also Abu al-Ḥusayn Muḥammad ibn Abi Ya'la, *Ṭabaqāt al-Ḥanābilah*, ed. Muḥammad al-Faqi, (Cairo, 1952), I, 284-286.

[6] Qur'ān III, 39.

[7] The Arabic equivalent of the English phrase "for the *kushkhar*" is transcribed correctly in the German edition as *lil-kushkhar*; in the Egyptian edition it is transcribed as *al-kushkhar*.

This much on the etymology and meaning of the word *iqlīm* is sufficient and efficacious, if it pleases God the Most High.

The various nations attribute four different meanings to the form and nature of the *aqālīm*:

The First Meaning

The first meaning, current among the vulgar and the mass of the people, is the one that is constantly on everyone's tongue. They call every district comprising a number of cities and villages an *iqlīm*, such as China, Khurāsān, Iraq, Syria, Egypt, and Ifrīqiyah (Tunisia), and so on. *Iqlīms*, according to this signification, are many and beyond count.

The Second Meaning

The second meaning is the one current among the people of al-Andalus, who call every large and populous village an *iqlīm*. It may be that this interpretation is known only to the distinguished among them. It is similar to that which we have quoted from Ḥamzah al-Iṣbahāni. Thus if an Andalusian says, "I am from such and such an *iqlīm*," he means a particular town or *rustāq*.

The Third Meaning

The third meaning, which is that of the Persians of old, is the one writers most frequently rely upon. Abu ar-Rayḥān has said:

> The Persians divided the kingdoms surrounding Īrānshahr into seven *kishwars*. They drew a circle around each kingdom and called it *kishwar* and *kushkhar*. Both of these terms, it has been said, are derived from *kushastah*, which is the word for 'line' in their language. It is known that circles of equal size do not surround one of their number that is tangent to all, unless they are seven in number, with six of them surrounding the seventh. [1]

Thus they divided Īrānshahr [2] into six *kishwars*, and the entire habitable world into seven. This division originated in that which Zoroaster, the founder of their religion, taught concerning the disposition of the earth and its division into seven parts, in the manner mentioned above. The central part, Hunayrah, [3] wherein we are, is surrounded by the other six.

Abu ar-Rayḥān has said:

> As regards the real reason for their dividing the oecumene into seven parts, I do not find myself capable of arriving at it by way of demonstrable proof. All those who concerned themselves with this matter did not incline to this view, save on the basis of the number of the planets, which they inferred from

[1] Only the first sentence of the above passage is found in the *Tafhīm*. A diagram showing the Persian division of the climes is given instead of the explanations contained in the rest of the above passage. See al-Bīrūni, *Tafhīm*, p. 142. Dr. Harold W. Glidden has drawn my attention to the fact that the Iranian concept of the seven *kishwars* is discussed in E. Herzfeld, *Zoroaster and His World*, (Princeton, 1947), II, 680-685.

[2] According to Yāqūt (*Muʿjam*, I, 417) this term is applied to the territory comprising Iraq, Fārs, al-Jibāl, and Khurāsān; according to Ibn Rustah (*B.G.A.*, VII, 103-109) it includes Khurāsān, Sijistān, Kirmān, Fārs, al-Ahwāz, al-Jibāl, Ādharbayjān, Armenia, Mosul, al-Jazīrah, Syria, and Iraq.

[3] This term appears as Khunīrath and Khunārath in Muḥammad ibn Jarīr aṭ-Ṭabari, *Taʾrīkh ar-Rusul w-al-Mulūk*, ed. De Geoje (Leyden, 1879-1898), I, 229 and II, 529. Al-Masʿūdi, who gives the name-form Khunīrath, maintains that it was a Chaldean or Syriac term that was widely used by Persians of all classes. See al-Masʿūdi, *B.G.A.*, VIII, 35. This word is from the Avestan *hvaniraθa*; see Herzfeld, *Zoroaster and His World*, II, 670, 802. (For the latter reference I am indebted to Dr. Harold W. Glidden.)

the number of days in a week.[1] There is no disagreement among the disputants of the nations concerning the days of the week or the principle laid down for their sequence, beginning with Sunday.

The image of the *kishwars* included within the *kushkhar* of Hunayrah is represented in the third diagram on the opposite page, [reproduced here below] as I copied it from the book of Abu ar-Rayḥān, done in his own hand.

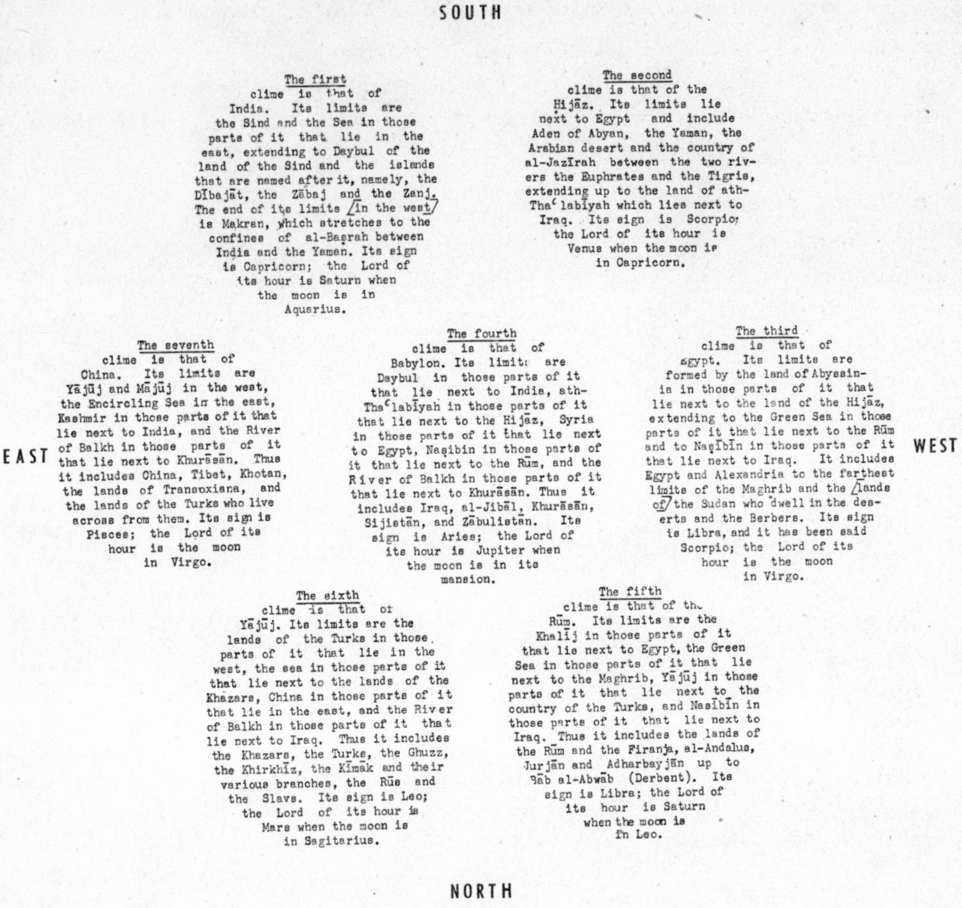
SOUTH
The first clime is that of India. Its limits are the Sind and the Sea in those parts of it that lie in the east, extending to Daybul of the land of the Sind and the islands that are named after it, namely, the Dībajāt, the Zābaj and the Zanj. The end of its limits [in the west] is Makran, which stretches to the confines of al-Baṣrah between India and the Yaman. Its sign is Capricorn; the Lord of its hour is Saturn when the moon is in Aquarius.
The second clime is that of the Ḥijāz. Its limits lie next to Egypt and include Aden of Abyan, the Yaman, the Arabian desert and the country of al-Jazīrah between the two rivers the Euphrates and the Tigris, extending up to the land of ath-Thaʿlabiyah which lies next to Iraq. Its sign is Scorpio; the Lord of its hour is Venus when the moon is in Capricorn.
The seventh clime is that of China. Its limits are Yājūj and Mājūj in the west, the Encircling Sea in the east, Kashmir in those parts of it that lie next to India, and the River of Balkh in those parts of it that lie next to Khurāsān. Thus it includes China, Tibet, Khotan, the lands of Transoxiana, and the lands of the Turks who live across from them. Its sign is Pisces; the Lord of its hour is the moon in Virgo.
EAST
The fourth clime is that of Babylon. Its limits are Daybul in those parts of it that lie next to India, ath-Thaʿlabīyah in those parts of it that lie next to the Ḥijāz, Syria in those parts of it that lie next to Egypt, Naṣibin in those parts of it that lie next to the Rūm, and the River of Balkh in those parts of it that lie next to Khurāsān. Thus it includes Iraq, al-Jibāl, Khurāsān, Sijistān, and Zābulistān. Its sign is Aries; the Lord of its hour is Jupiter when the moon is in its mansion.
The third clime is that of Egypt. Its limits are formed by the land of Abyssinia in those parts of it that lie next to the land of the Ḥijāz, extending to the Green Sea in those parts of it that lie next to the Rūm and to Naṣībīn in those parts of it that lie next to Iraq. It includes Egypt and Alexandria to the farthest limits of the Maghrib and the [lands of] the Sudan who dwell in the deserts and the Berbers. Its sign is Libra, and it has been said Scorpio; the Lord of its hour is the moon in Virgo.
WEST
The sixth clime is that of Yājūj. Its limits are the lands of the Turks in those parts of it that lie in the west, the sea in those parts of it that lie next to the lands of the Khazars, China in those parts of it that lie in the east, and the River of Balkh in those parts of it that lie next to Iraq. Thus it includes the Khazars, the Turks, the Ghuzz, the Khirkhīz, the Kīmāk and their various branches, the Rūs and the Slavs. Its sign is Leo; the Lord of its hour is Mars when the moon is in Sagitarius.
The fifth clime is that of the Rūm. Its limits are the Khalīj in those parts of it that lie next to Egypt, the Green Sea in those parts of it that lie next to the Maghrib, Yājūj in those parts of it that lie next to the country of the Turks, and Naṣībīn in those parts of it that lie next to Iraq. Thus it includes the lands of the Rūm and the Firanja, al-Andalus, Jurjān and Adharbayjān up to Bāb al-Abwāb (Derbent). Its sign is Libra; the Lord of its hour is Saturn when the moon is in Leo.
NORTH

Fig. 3.

Yāqūt evidently copied this diagram from al-Bīrūni's *Taḥdīd Nihāyāt al-Amākin li-Taṣḥīḥ Masāfāt al-Masākin.* For the wording of al-Bīrūni's text which appears within the seven circles representing the seven climes is substantially the same as that of Yāqūt, although it is briefer and does not have the astrological information found in Yāqūt. See *Biruni's Picture of the World,* ed. A. Zeki Velidi Togan (Delhi 1934), p. 61.

Note: In the above diagram, the place name az-Zābaj, in the first clime, appears erroneously as ar-Rānaj. The text in the circle representing the second clime appears to be corrupt. In the seventh clime, the text has the phrase, *w-al-Atrāk al muḥāribah lahum* (the Turks who fight against them) which has been changed to read, *w-al-Atrāk al-muḥādhiyah lahum* (the Turks who live across from them), as it appears in A. Z. Velidi Togan's *Biruni's Picture of the World.*

[1] It will be noted that the above passage is not very clear. It probably means that the idea of the seven climes was based upon the number of the seven planets following the example of the seven-day week, which itself had originally been based upon the same. Cf. al-Bīrūni, *Tafhīm,* pp. 237-238 and al-Bīrūni, *India,* I, 213.

Abu ar-Rayḥān said:

> Hermes upheld this division, according to that which Muḥammad ibn Ibrāhīm al-Fazāri [1] attributed to him in his *Zīj* (astronomical tables). Since Hermes was one of the ancients, it appears that in his time no other division was used; otherwise, matters pertaining to mathematics and astronomy were more particularly within the province of Hermes. [2]

Abu ar-Rayḥān continued:

> al-Fazāri added, 'Each *kishwar* is 700 *farsakhs* by 700 *farsakhs*.' [3]

I have read elsewhere than in Abu ar-Rayḥān's book that each of these seven *iqlīms*, which we have described above, extends lengthwise for 700 *farsakhs*, except for the seventh, which extends for 220 *farsakhs*. But God is the most knowing.

The Fourth Meaning

The fourth meaning is the one relied upon by mathematicians, philosophers, and astronomers. The *iqlīm*, according to them, extends lengthwise from east to west, as we shall show in a diagram later. After mentioning the signification used by the people of Fārs, Abu ar-Rayḥān said the following, which I have copied from his own handwriting:

> As regards one who has practiced the art of astronomy and has been enamored of cosmography, he has approached this division from a different point of view. He examined the first division and found it to lack a system of natural, rather than artificial causes, which it consistently follows and in accordance with which various regions of the globe differ as to heat and cold and other characteristics. Whereupon he turned away from that division and heeded it not.

He then said:

> If we were to contemplate the changes that attend night and day as a result of the entrance of one into the other, at both ends of the summer and winter—the intense heat and severe cold which occur in the air, and their effects upon the land and the water—we should find after careful observation that these two [changes] are in accordance with the two directions of north and south.
>
> If in going toward the east or the west we were to keep to one latitude, the following of which would not bring us any closer to the north or to the south, we should experience no change whatsoever in so far as the atmosphere is concerned. However, change does take place as a result of a transition from the *ṣurūd* (cold upland regions) to the *jurūm* (warm lowland regions), or vice versa,—a change not caused by moving along the same latitude, but rather caused by the highlands and the lowlands and the dissimilar conditions prevailing therein, as well as by the early and late risings and settings of the sun. These facts are not discoverable through the senses, but are arrived at through observation and measurement.
>
> Thus if we were to divide the oecumene latitudinally, according to the differences and changes therein, into parallel sections along the extension of the land so that every part in the east and in the west would be in approxi-

[1] Astronomer of the 8th century A.D. He is said to have translated the Indian *Siddhānta* for the Caliph al-Manṣūr. See Nallino, "Storia dell' astronomia," *Raccolta*, V, 209-218; Sarton, *History of Science*, I, 530.

[2] This passage is cited by Nallino, who refers to Yāqūt as one of those who have attributed the *Zīj* to al-Fazāri. See Nallino, "Storia dell' astronomia," *Raccolta*, V, 211.

[3] Cf. Ibn al-Faqīh who states, "Hermes alleged that the dimensions of each *iqlīm* are 700 *farsakhs* by 700." See Ibn al-Faqīh, *B.G.A.*, V. 7.

mately the same state, this would be more sound than dividing it in any other manner.

He then contemplated the longest and the shortest day, and since the one is the counterpart of the other, they are investigated in the same manner. He found the longest day to be 13 hours in the North, where people are civilized and on the whole moderate in physical appearance and in character. They are unlike the savages, hiding in forests and wildernesses, who tear to pieces and devour those persons whom they chance upon. He placed the southern limit of the longest

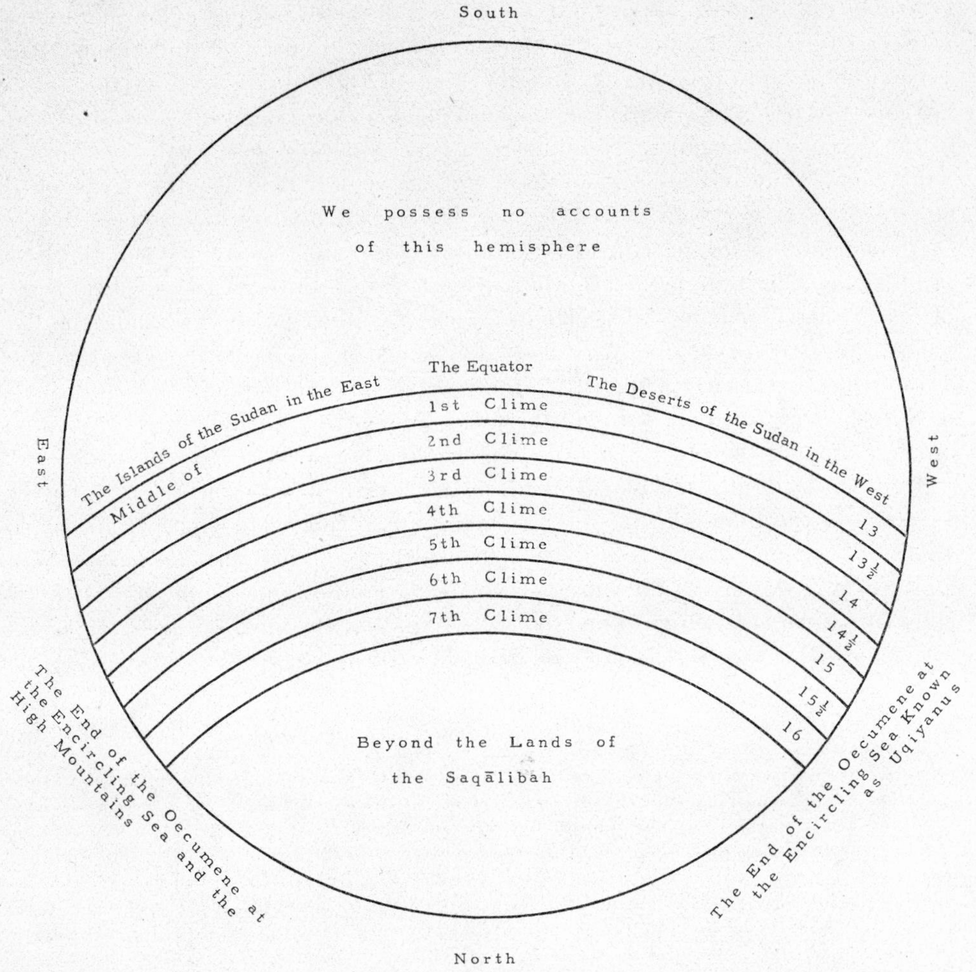

Fig. 4.

day in the middle of the first clime and the northern limit in the middle of the seventh clime. In the middle of each of the remaining climes the longest day is increased by half an hour. As regards that which lies beyond the seventh clime, it consists of lands where cold occurs in summer and is devastating in winter, and where winter is the longest season of the year. Consequently, the inhabitants of these parts are few and they are mentally deficient. Their bestiality is such that they perhaps would be loath to mingle with people as they, brute-like, view them from beyond the seventh clime . . . [1]

[1] Cf. al-Bīrūni, *Tafhīm*, pp. 137-138, where the author discusses the longest day and gives a table showing the increase of the longest day by half an hour from the middle of one clime to another.

If you were then to divide the oecumene into climes in this manner, its image would approximate the fourth diagram on the opposite page [here on p. 43].[1]

The First Clime

The first clime begins where the meridian shadow—when the day and night are equal—is one, one-half, one-tenth, and one-sixth of one-tenth feet. It ends where the equinoctial shadow at the meridian is two and three-fifths feet.

It begins in the east, from the farthest limit of the country of China, and stretches over the southern extension thereof. In it is the island of Ceylon (Sarandīb). It stretches across the seacoast in the south of the country of Sind. Then it traverses the sea towards Arabia and the land of the Yaman, crosses the Sea of Qulzum towards the country of Abyssinia, passes over Egypt's Nile, and ends in the Sea of the Maghrib. The middle of this clime lies close to the territory of Ṣanʿāʾ and Ḥaḍramawt. Its southern extremity lies close to the territory of Aden, while its northern extremity lies close to Tihāmah, which is near Mecca.

Among the flourishing lands that lie in the first clime are the city of the King of China, southern Sind, the island of al-Kark,[2] and southern India; of the lands of the Yaman: Ṣanʿāʾ, Aden, Ḥaḍramawt, Najrān, Jurāsh, Jayshān, Ṣaʿdah, Sabaʾ, Ẓufār, Mahrah, and ʿUmān; of the lands of the Maghrib: Tabālah; also Jarmī, the capital city of the ruler of Abyssinia, and Dumqalah, the capital city of Nubia;[3] the territory of the southern Berbers; Ghānah, which is in the country of the Sūdān of the Maghrib; and then the Green Sea.

The longest day in the places mentioned is 12½ hours where the clime begins, 13 hours in the middle of it, and 13¼ hours at its end.[4] Its length from east to west is 9,772 miles and 41 minutes, its width 442 miles and 22 minutes and 40 seconds. Its area amounts to 4,320,877 square miles and 21 minutes. It is the clime of Saturn, a fact upon which both Persians and Byzantines agree. In Persian it is called Kaywān. Capricorn and Aquarius are its signs.

[1] Yāqūt's description of the climes and his enumeration of places follows an older tradition. For notwithstanding some variations, Yāqūt's text has much in common with a number of earlier texts. Minorsky (*Sharaf Al-Zamān Ṭāhir Marvazi on China, the Turks and India*, [London, 1942], pp. 63-64) has pointed out the similarity that exists between Al-Farghāni, *Fi al-Ḥarakāt as-Samāwīyah*, p. 35; Ibn Rustah, *B.G.A.*, VII, 96-98; al-Muṭahhar, *Kitāb al-Badʾ w-at-Taʾrīkh*, IV, 49-53; *Mujmal at-Tawārīkh*, pp. 479-481; Minorsky, *Marvazi*, pp. 13-14; and Yāqūt. Other earlier texts similar to Yāqūt are al-Maqdisi, *B.G.A.*, III, 59-61, and al-Bīrūni, *Tafhīm*, pp. 143-146. Al-Qazwīni offers an interesting example for comparison. Of special interest to us is the information with which al-Qazwīni prefaces each of the seven climes. Here he gives the length of the meridian shadow at the beginning and at the end of each clime; the length of the longest day at the beginning, the middle, and the end of each clime; and the dimensions of the climes. Apart from a few discrepancies, due to the error of the copyist, his dependence upon Yāqūt is quite obvious. His text follows that of Yāqūt to the extent of reproducing all the errors and discrepancies that appear in Yāqūt. Cf. *Kitāb Āthār al-Bilād wa-Akhbār al-ʿIbād*, ed. F. Wüstenfeld, (Göttingen, 1848), pp. 9, 48, 92, 188, 331, 387, and 411.

[2] Thus vocalized in Yāqūt's text. Minorsky transcribes it as al-K.rk and gives the different forms in which this place name appears in various authors. See Minorsky, *Marvazi*, p. 64.

[3] This name, which appears erroneously as an-Nabwah in the Egyptian edition, should be restored to an-Nūbah (Nubia) as in the German edition.

[4] The length of the longest day at the beginning of the first clime should be 12¾ hours, as in al-Bīrūni, *Tafhīm*, p. 138, instead of 12½ hours as above. For the increase in the length of the longest day from the middle of one clime to the middle of another is half an hour. Al-Qazwīni, (*Āthār al-Bilād*, p. 9) gives the same figures as Yāqūt.

The Second Clime

The second clime begins where the equinoctial shadow—when the day and night are equal—is two and three-fifths feet at the meridian. It ends where the equinoctial shadow at the meridian is three, one-half, and one-tenth of one-sixth feet. [1]

It begins in the east, and passes over China and India, and over the northern parts of the latter, namely Qāmrūn, Kanūj, and Sind. Thence it stretches over the confluence of the Green Sea and the Sea of Basrah, and traverses Arabia, passing over the lands of Najd, Tihāmah, and al-Baḥrayn. It then crosses the Sea of Qulzum and Egypt's Nile towards the lands of the Maghrib.

The cities that lie in this clime are those of China, India and Sind, wherein is al-Manṣūrah, the lands of the Tatars, and Daybul. It traverses the sea towards the land of the Arabs in the direction of ʿUmān. In the middle of this clime lies Yathrib, the city of the Prophet. Its [2] farthest southern limits lie a little beyond Mecca, while its farthest northern limits lie close to ath-Thaʿlabīyah. Both Mecca and ath-Thaʿlabīyah partake of two climes, as do all places that lie on their latitudes.

Among the famous lands that lie in this clime are Mecca, al-Madīnah, Fayd, ath-Thaʿlabīyah, al-Yamāmah, Hajar, Tabālah, aṭ-Ṭā'if, Jidda, the kingdom of Abyssinia; and the land of Bujah; of the land of the Nile: Qūṣ, Ikhmīm, Anṣinā, and Aswān; of western territories: Tunisia and certain of the mountains of the Berbers, as far as the land of the Maghrib.

The longest day in the places mentioned is $13\frac{1}{4}$ hours where the clime begins, $13\frac{1}{2}$ hours in the middle of it, and $13\frac{3}{4}$ hours at its end. Its length from east to west is 9,312 miles and 42 minutes, its width 402 miles and 51 minutes. Its area is 3,690,340 square miles and 54 minutes. It is the clime of Jupiter, according to the Persians; according to the Byzantines, it is the clime of the Sun. Its name in Persian is Hurmuz. Sagittarius and Pisces are its signs. All that which is on its latitude, to the east and to the west, is included within it.

The Third Clime

The third clime begins where the meridian shadow—when the day and night are equal—is three, one-half, one-tenth, and one-sixth of one-tenth feet. [3] It ends where the equinoctial shadow in the meridian is four, one-half, and one-third of one-tenth feet. In the middle of the third clime the day attains a length of 14 hours. This clime begins in the east, passing over northern China, India,

[1] The length of the meridian shadow at the end of the second clime does not agree with the length of the meridian shadow at the beginning of the third clime, which is given as, "three, one-half, one-tenth, and one-sixth of one-tenth," both by Yāqūt and by al-Maqdisi. Since the length of the meridian shadow is the same at the end of one clime and at the beginning of the next clime, the above figures for the length of the meridian shadow at the end of the second clime must be due to an error. Al-Qazwīni, *Āthār al-Bilād*, p. 48, gives the same figures as Yāqūt for the length of the meridian shadow at the end of the second clime.

[2] It should be pointed out here that in both the German and the Egyptian editions the Arabic preposition *fi* (in) occurs needlessly and erroneously in the above sentence. The original text reads: " 'In' its farthest limits lie a little beyond Mecca etc.," instead of as above where the preposition "in" has been omitted. This error, which occurs more than once in the section on the climes, is corrected with no further reference being made to it.

[3] Probably due to a copyist's mistake the length of the meridian shadow at the end of the third clime is given in al-Qazwīni, *Āthār al-Bilād*, p. 92 as: "four, one-half, two-tenths, and one-third of one-tenth feet."

Sind, Kābul, Kirmān, Sijistān, Fārs, al-Ahwāz, the Two Iraqs,[1] Syria, Cairo, and Alexandria. Among the cities located in this clime, beyond China, is Wāqiṣah on the edge of Iraq; it lies in the middle of the clime, which is near Madyan on the edge of Syria. Ath-Thaʿlabīyah and all places in this latitude, to the east and to the west, lie within its southernmost limits. Baghdad, the City of Peace, Fārs, Qandahār,[2] India, Multān in the land of Sind, Nihāyah,[3] Karūr, the Afghan Mountains, Tyre of Syria, Tiberias, and Beirut lie within its northernmost limits. Likewise, all places in this latitude, to the east and to the west, partake of two climes.

Among the well-known cities that lie in this clime are Ghaznah, Kābul, ar-Rukhkhaj[4] (Arachosia), the mountains of Zābulistān, Sijistān, Iṣbahān, Bust, Zaranj, and Kirmān; of Fārs: Iṣṭakhr, Jūr,[5] Fasā, Sābūr, Shīrāz, Sīrāf, Jannābah, Sīnīz, Mahrūbān, and all the districts of al-Ahwāz; of Iraq: al-Baṣrah, Wāsiṭ, al-Kūfah, Baghdad, al-Anbār, Hīt, and al-Jazīrah; of Syria: Ḥimṣ, according to certain accounts, and Damascus, Tyre, Acre, Tiberias, Caesarea, Arsūf, ar-Ramlah, Jerusalem, Ascalon, Gaza, Madyan, and Qulzum; of the land of Egypt: Faramā, Tinnīs, Damietta, al-Fusṭāṭ, Alexandria, al-Fayyūm; of the Maghrib: Barqah, Tunisia (Ifrīqīyah), al-Qayrawān, the tribes of the Berbers in the lands of the west, Tāhart, Sūs, and the land of Tangier, and then it ends in the Encircling Sea.

The longest day in the places mentioned as $13\frac{3}{4}$ hours where the clime begins, 14 hours in the middle of it, and $14\frac{1}{4}$ hours at its end. Its length from east to west is 8,774 miles[6] and 23 minutes, its width 348 miles and 45 minutes. Its area is 3,006,458 square miles and 29 minutes. It is the clime of Mars, according to the Persians; according to the Byzantines, it is the clime of Mercury. Its name in Persian is Bahrām. Aries and Scorpio are its signs. All that which is on its latitude is included within it.

And God grants assistance in the attainment of what is right.

[1] al-Kūfah and al-Baṣrah. See *Muʿjam* III, 628. In later times this term came to be applied to lower Mesopotamia and the Jibāl province of Iran, which were referred to as al-ʿIrāq al-ʿArabi and al-ʿIrāq al-ʿAjami. See article "Al-ʿIrāḳ" by M. Hartmann in *E. I.*

[2] The above place name is given in al-Maqdisi (*B.G.A.*, III, 59) as *Qandahār al-Hind*, i.e. "the Qandahār of India." This is most probably the port of Ghandhār India. According to Gibb, Qandahār is an arabicization of Gandhar or Gundhar, known to medieval seamen as Gandar, a port located on the estuary of the small river Dhandar. See Ibn Battuta, *Travels in Asia and Africa*: 1325-1354, trans. and ed. H. A .R. Gibb, (New York, 1932) p. 363, note 10.

[3] The above word appears in the German edition in the following context: *wa-min arḍ as-Sind al-Multān wa-nihāyatuhu* etc., i.e. "and of the land of Sind, Multān and its borders etc."; in the Egyptian edition it appears as Nihāyah. Wüstenfeld indicates in the "Anmerkungen," *Muʿjam,* V, 2 that Khanikov's Mashhad Codex gives it as Nihāyah, while the Berlin Codex of the Sprenger collection and Rousseau's St. Petersburg Codex give it as Tihāmah. The same word appears in al-Bīrūni, *Tafhīm,* p. 144, as Nihāyah and is restored by Wright to Tihāmah.

[4] According to Minorsky, early Muslim geographers refer to the region of the present-day Qandahār as ar-Rukhkhaj and place its capital at Panjway. See Minorsky, *Marvazi,* p. 152, note 3.

[5] Jūr is the arabicized form of the Persian name Gūr (grave). This name was deemed inauspicious by the courtiers of ʿAḍud ad-Dawlah the Buwayhid, who liked the town and was there often, so they decided to change it to Fīrūzābād, or the "Abode of Luck." See Le Strange, *Lands of the Eastern Caliphate,* pp. 255-256.

[6] Apparently due to a copyist's error the length of this clime is given as 800,774 miles in both the German and the Egyptian editions. The same error is found in al-Qazwīni, *Āthār al-Bilād,* p. 92.

The Fourth Clime

The fourth clime begins where the meridian shadow in the month of March —when the day and night are equal—is four, three-fifths, and one-third of one-fifth feet. [1] It ends where the meridian shadow at the equinox is five, three-fifths, and one-third of one-fifth feet. It begins in the lands of China, Tibet, and Khotan, and includes those cities that lie between them. It passes over the mountains of Kashmīr, Bolor, Burjān, Badhakhshān, Kābul, Ghūr, Harāt, Balkh, Ṭukhāristān, Marv, Qūhistān, Nīsābūr, Qūmis, Jurjān, Ṭabaristān, ar-Rayy, Qumm, Qāshān, Hamadhān, Adharbayjān, Mosul, Ḥarrān, ʿAzāz, ath-Thughūr [2] (the frontier fortresses), the islands of Cyprus, Rhodes, and Sicily, and thence to the Encircling Sea, passing over the Straits between Spain and the lands of the Maghrib. The southernmost reaches of this clime lie near Baghdad, where it passes over Iraq, and in all places, to the east and to the west, that are on its latitude. Its northernmost reaches lie near Qālīqalā [3] (Erzerum) and along the shores of Ṭabaristān to Ardabīl, Jurjān, and all places that lie on this latitude.

Among the renowned cities located in this clime, other than those mentioned, are Naṣībīn, Dārā, the two Raqqahs [4] (ar-Raqqah and ar-Rāfiqah), Ra'ṣ al-ʿAyn, Sumaysāṭ (Samosata), ar-Ruhā (Edessa), Manbij (Hierapolis), Aleppo, Qinnasrīn, Antioch, Ḥimṣ (Emesa)—according to a certain account—al-Maṣṣīṣah (Mopsuestia), Adhanah (Adana), Ṭarsūs, Surra-man-ra'a (Sāmarrā'), Ḥulwān, Shahrazūr, Māsabadhān, Dīnawar, Nahāwand, Iṣbahān, Marāghah, Zinjān, Qazwīn, Karkh, Sarakhs, Iṣṭakhr (Persepolis), Ṭūs, Marv ar-Rūdh, Sidon, al-Kanīsah as-Sawdā' [5] (the Black Church), Amorium, and Latakia.

The longest day in the places mentioned is $14\frac{1}{4}$ hours where the clime begins, $14\frac{1}{2}$ hours in the middle of it, and $14\frac{3}{4}$ hours at its end. Its length from east to west is 8,214 miles and 14 minutes, its width 299 miles and 4 minutes. Its area is 1,473,072 square miles and 22 minutes. It is the clime of the Sun, according to the Persians; according to the Byzantines, it is the clime of Jupiter. Its name in Persian is Khurshādh. Leo is its sign.

And God is the dispenser of assistance.

The Fifth Clime

The fifth clime begins where the meridian shadow—when the day and night are equal—is five, three-fifths, and one-sixth of one-fifth feet. [6] Its middle is where the meridian shadow at the equinox is six feet, and it ends where the

[1] The above figures for the length of the meridian shadow at the beginning of the fourth clime do not agree with the figures given for the length of the meridian shadow at the end of the Third Clime. The same discrepancy is found in al-Maqdisi, *B.G.A.*, III, 60 and in al-Qazwīni, *Āthār al-Bilād*, p. 188.

[2] The zone of frontier fortresses built against the Byzantines in the Syrian and Mesopotamian marches. See article "Al-Thughūr" by E. Honigmann in *E. I.*, and Le Strange, *Lands of the Eastern Caliphate*, p. 128.

[3] The Armenian Karin-Kʿatakʿ. See Minorsky, *Ḥudūd*, p. 395.

[4] Twin cities situated above where the river Balīkh empties into the Euphrates. The older town of ar-Raqqah occupied the site of the Greek city of Callinicus or Nicephorium; ar-Rāfiqah was built by the Caliph al-Manṣūr in A.H. 155/A.D. 772. See Le Strange, *Lands of the Eastern Caliphate*, pp. 101-103.

[5] An ancient fortress built of black stone. Its exact position is not known, but it is supposed to have been located between Marʿash (Germanicia) and ʿAyn Zarbah. See *ibid.*, pp. 128-130.

[6] The length of the meridian shadow at the beginning of the fifth clime does not agree with the length of the meridian shadow at the end of the fourth clime. This discrepancy is found in al-Maqdisi, *B.G.A.*, III, 61 and al-Qazwīni, *Āthār al-Bilād*, p. 331.

meridian shadow, to the east or to the west, is six, one-half of one-tenth, and one-sixth of one-tenth feet. Its width, according to one account, is about 130 miles.

It begins in the land of the eastern Turks and the territory of Gog (Yājūj), the walled-in, and passes over the lands of various kinds of Turks, who are known by their tribes, to Kāshghar, Balāṣāghūn, [1] Zāsht, [2] Farghānah, Isbījāb, [3] Shāsh (Tashkent), Ushrūsanah, [4] Samarqand, Bukhāra, Khwārizm, the Sea of the Khazars (the Caspian Sea), to Bāb al-Abwāb (Derbent), Bardha'ah, Mayyāfāriqīn (Martyropolis), Armenia, Durūb ar-Rūm (the roads of the Byzantines) [5] and their country. It passes over Rūmīyah al-Kubra (Rome), the land of the Jalāliqah (Galicians), and the land of Spain, and ends in the Encircling Sea. Its middle lies near the land of Tiflīs in the country of Armenia, and near Jurjān and all cities, to the east and to the west, which lie on this latitude. Its southernmost reaches lie near Khilāṭ, Dabīl, Sumaysāṭ (Samosata), Malaṭyah (Melitene), 'Ammūriyah (Amorium), and all places, to the east and to the west, that lie on this latitude. Its northernmost reaches lie near Dabīl. The cities of Gog and Magog (Yājūj wa-Mājūj) lie within its latitude.

The longest day in the places mentioned is $14\frac{3}{4}$ hours at the beginning of the clime, 15 hours in the middle of it, and $15\frac{1}{4}$ hours at its end. The length of this clime at its middle, from east to west, is 7,670 miles and several tens of minutes; its width is 254 miles and 30 minutes. Its area is 1,048,584 square miles and 12 minutes. It is the clime of Venus, a fact upon which both Persians and Byzantines agree. Its name in Persian is Anāhīd. Taurus and Libra are its signs.

The Sixth Clime

The sixth clime begins where the meridian shadow at the equinox is seven, six-tenths, and one-sixth of one-tenth feet. [6] Its end exceeds its beginning by

[1] This place name appears erroneously as al-Iṣīfūn in both the German and the Egyptian editions. Balāṣāghūn is a town in Sogdiana, whose location cannot now be exactly determined. See article "Balāṣāg͟hūn" by W. Barthold in *E. I.*

[2] This place name is given as Zāsht in both the German and the Egyptian editions. Wüstenfeld, however, seems to favor the reading Rāsht. See "Anmerkungen," *Mu'jam*, V, 3. Minorsky, who states that the usual reading is Rāsht, discusses the two readings and points out that both the anonymous author of *Ḥūdūd al-'Ālam* and Gardīzi spell the word as Zāsht. He also refers to Ya'qūbi's spelling, which he describes as "a good parallel for Zāsht." According to Minorsky, Yāqūt mentions separately both Rāsht (*Mu'jam*, II, 733) and Zāsht (*Mu'jam*, II, 907) but fails to give any clue as to the location of the latter. For further details see Minorsky, *Ḥudūd*, p. 361.

[3] The site of medieval Isbījāb is now occupied by the present-day Sayram, which lies on the Arīs or Bodan river, a right-bank affluent of the Jaxartes. It is located about eight miles to the east of Chimkant. See Le Strange, *Lands of the Eastern Caliphate*, pp. 483-484 and Minorsky, *Ḥudūd*, pp. 357-358.

[4] The name of a province in Transoxiana. This name has several readings viz. Ushrūsanah, Usrūshanah, Surūshanah and Surūshnah. According to Kramers the name-form Usrūshanah is the best known, although Yāqūt (*Mu'jam*, I, 245) prefers Ushrūsanah. Minorsky, like Kramers, seems to favor the reading Usrūshanah. This province lay between the Sughd river and the Jaxartes on the slopes of the Buttamān mountains. The site of the capital of this province, Būnjikath, is identical with the present-day Uratepeh. See Le Strange, *Lands of the Eastern Caliphate*, pp. 474-475, article "Osrūs͟hana" by J. H Kramers in *E. I.*, Minorsky, *Ḥudūd*, p. 354.

[5] Roads or passes leading into the lands of the Byzantines, especially those leading through the Cilician Gates (Pylae Ciliciae) from Tarsus by way of Badhandun (Podandos) and Lu'lu'ah (Loulon) to Tyana and Heraclia, and the eastern route from Mar'ash by way of Ḥadath to Malaṭyah. See article "Darb" by R. Hartmann in *E. I.*

[6] The length of the meridian shadow at the beginning of the sixth clime is one foot too long and consequently does not agree with the length of the meridian shadow at the end

only one foot. It begins in the homelands of the Turks of the East, such as Qāy,[1] Qūn,[2] Khirkhīz,[3] Kīmāk,[4] Toghuzghuz; the lands of the Turkomans, Fārāb, the country of the Khazars, and to the north of the Khazar Sea, the land of the Alans, the Sarīr, which are between the Khazar Sea and the Sea of Ṭarābzundah (the Black Sea). It passes over Constantinople, the land of the Franks, and northern Spain, until it ends in the Western Sea. The width of this clime, according to some accounts, is 200 and some odd miles. Its southernmost limits are conterminous with the northernmost limits of the fifth clime,[5] while its northernmost limits lie near the land of Khwārizm, and beyond Ṭurārband[6] of Shāsh, which adjoins the land of the Turks. Its middle lies near Constantinople, Āmul of Khurāsān, and Farghānah. There lie in this clime, according to some accounts, many of the cities mentioned in the fifth clime, as well as others. The latter include Samarqand, Bāb al-Khazar (Derbent), al-Jīl (Gīlān), the northern parts of Spain, the southern parts of the country of the Slavs, and Heraclea.

The longest day in the places mentioned is 15½ hours at the beginning of the clime,[7] and 15¾ hours at its end. The length of this clime at its middle, from east to west, is 7,175 miles and 63 minutes. Its width is 215 miles and 39 minutes. Its area is 1,046,721 square miles and some minutes.

of the fifth clime. Al-Qazwīni (*Āthār al-Bilād*, p. 387) gives the same figures as Yāqūt. Al-Maqdisi (*B.G.A.*, III, 62) comes much closer to the correct figures. The length of the meridian shadow at the beginning of the sixth clime according to al-Maqdisi is as follows: Six, six-tenths, and one-sixth of one-tenth feet.

1 Both the German and the Egyptian editions have Qāni, although both the Berlin Codex of the Sprenger collection and Rousseau's St. Petersburg Codex have Qāy. See "Anmerkungen," *Muʿjam*, V, 3. The name Qāni has been restored to Qāy in comformity with other texts where it occurs, namely: al-Bīrūni, *Tafhīm*, p. 145, Minorsky, *Marvazi*, pp. 29-30, al-Kāshghari, *Dīwān Lughāt at-Turk*, I, 28. It is interesting in this connection to note Minorsky's observation that al-Kāshghari makes a distinction between Qāy and Qāyigh (al-Kāshghari, *ibid.*, I, 56) and that M. F. Köprülü-Zade has also insisted on this distinction. He therefore suggests that Yāqūt's Qāni may reflect Qāyigh rather than Qāy. See Minorsky, *Ḥudūd*, p. 285.

2 For a discussion of Qāy and Qūn see Minorsky, *Marvazi*, pp. 95-100.

3 A Turkish people. See article "Kirgiz" by W. Barthold in *E. I.*, and Minorsky, *Ḥudūd*, pp. 282-286.

4 A Turkish people. See article "Kīmak" by W. Barthold in *E. I.*, and Minorsky, *Ḥudūd*, pp. 304-310.

5 Yāqūt's text as it appears in both the German and the Egyptian editions is corrupt at this point. The text has been corrected in accordance with Fleischer's suggestion ("Anmerkungen," *Muʿjam*, V, 3), which comes very close to a parallel passage in al-Maqdisi, *B.G.A.*, III, 62.

6 Obviously due to a copyist's mistake the above place-name appears as Ṭarābzundah in both the German and the Egyptian editions. It should be pointed out here that different authors have spelled this name differently. It appears as aṭ-Ṭurārband in Ibn al-Faqīh, *B.G.A.*, V, 322, as Ṭurārband in al-Maqdisi, *B.G.A.*, III, p. 61, and in Ibn Rustah, *B.G.A.*, VII, p. 98, as Ṭarband in the Arabic text of Muṭahhar, *Kitāb al-Badʾ w-at-Taʾrīkh*, IV. Yāqūt discusses the name in two places, under the entry "Uṭrār" (*Muʿjam*, I, 310) where he states that both name-forms Uṭrār and Utrār are correct, and under the entry "Ṭurārband" (*ibid.*, III, 524), where he states that this name may be read as Ṭurār or Utrār. Barthold has pointed out that the name of Utrār is met with as early as aṭ-Ṭabari (*Taʾrīkh ar-Rusul w-al-Mulūk* II, 816), who mentions the prince of the town of Utrārbanda among the enemies of the Caliph al-Maʾmūn. See Barthold, *Turkistan*, p. 61. This town, which was located near Fārāb, is now in ruins. It was here that Tīmūr Lang died in 1405. For further details see article "Otrār" by J. H. Kramers in *E. I.*

7 The number of hours in the longest day at the beginning of the sixth clime is incorrect. The day in question should be 15¼ hours long, which figure corresponds with the number of hours in the longest day at the end of the fifth clime. The same error is found in al-Qazwīni, *Āthār al-Bilād*, p. 387. It is evident from the foregoing that 15½ hours represents the longest day in the middle, rather than at the beginning, of this clime.

It is the clime of Mercury, according to the Persians; according to the Byzantines, it is the clime of the Moon. Its name in Persian is Tīr. Gemini and Virgo are its signs.

The Seventh Clime

The seventh clime begins where the meridian shadow at the equinox is seven, one-half, one-tenth, and one-sixth of one-tenth feet, as it is in the sixth clime. [1] For the end of the sixth clime is the beginning of this one. It ends where the meridian shadow at the equinox is eight, one-half, and one-half of one-tenth feet. There is not much habitation in this clime, for in the east it is but forests and mountains in which bands of savage-like Turks take shelter. It passes over the mountains of Bāshghird, the limits of the country of the Pechenegs, the towns of Sūwār [2] and Bulghār, [3] and the lands of the Rūs, Slavs, and Bulghārs, ending in the Encircling Sea.

There are a few nations beyond this clime, such as the Īsū, [4] the Warānk (Varangians), the Yūrah, [5] and so on. Its southernmost limits lie along the northernmost limits of the sixth clime, which adjoins it. This is the latitude of Khwārizm and Ṭurārband, to the east and to the west. Its northernmost limits lie in the remotest lands of the Slavs in the east and in the territories of the Turks adjoining Khwārizm to the north. Its middle passes through the land of the Alans. There are no well-known cities worthy of mention in this clime.

The longest day in the places mentioned is 15¾ hours at the beginning of the clime, 16 hours in the middle of it, and 16¼ hours at its end. The length of this clime at its middle, from east to west, is 6,780 miles and 54 minutes, its width 185 miles and 20 minutes. Its area is 1,224,824 square miles and 49 minutes.

It is the clime of the Moon, according to the Persians; according to the Byzantines, it is the clime of Mars. Its name in Persian is Māh, and Cancer is its sign. The end of this clime marks the end of the oecumene, beyond which no one is

[1] The length of the meridian shadow at the beginning of the seventh clime does not agree with the length of the meridian shadow at the end of the sixth clime, which was erroneously increased by one foot (see footnote 6, p. 48). Al-Qazwīni's figures are again like Yāqūt's except for some fractional discrepancy, which is probably due to a copyist's error.

[2] In both the German and the Egyptian editions this place name is erroneously transcribed as Surār.

[3] According to Minorsky (*Ḥudūd*, p. 461), the ruins of Bulghār are located near the village of Bolgarskoye or Uspenskoye, in the Spassk district 115 km. south of Kazan and at a distance of 7 km. from the left bank of the Volga. The town of Suwār on the other hand was located on the river Utka near the present village of Kuznechikha. For further details see article "Bulghār" by W. Barthold in *E. I.*

[4] According to Minorsky (*Marvazi*, p. 113) the Wīsū have been identified with the Finnish Ves (Veps) since the time of Fraehn. The *Russian Chronicles* place this people near Belozero, and their descendants are still found between Lakes Onega and Ladoga. Minorsky (*ibid*, note 1), refers to M.V. Talitsky, who maintains that the Īsū as described by Gharnāṭi, ʿAwfi, and Yāqūt should be located on the upper Kama. It appears that R. Hennig (see *Ḥudūd*, pp. 436-437, note 2), who places the Īsū in the neighborhood of Cherdin on the Kama, is of the same opinion. Minorsky, however, believes that a question of this nature can be settled only after a thorough investigation of all available sources. See Minorsky, *Marvazi*, pp. 112-113.

[5] The term Yūrah is identical with the Russian Yugra according to Minorsky. He cites the opinion of Prof. S. V. Bakhrushin to the effect that in the eleventh century the Novgorodians applied the name Yugra to the Ugrian people, who lived between the Pechora river and the Ural mountains. The term Yugra appears to have been applied to certain tribes which later came to be known as Ostiak. Among the latter lived some Vogul tribes. See Minorsky, *Marvazi*, pp. 113-114.

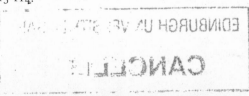

to be found save a people of no consequence. In their impoverished state and lack of refinement, they are more like wild beasts than men.

And God grants assistance in the attainment of what is right.

On Cities Belonging to Each of the Twelve Signs of the Zodiac

Aries has Babylon, Fārs, Adharbayjān, the territory of the Alāns, and Palestine.

Taurus has the Māhān, Hamadhān, the territory of the Kurdish highlanders,

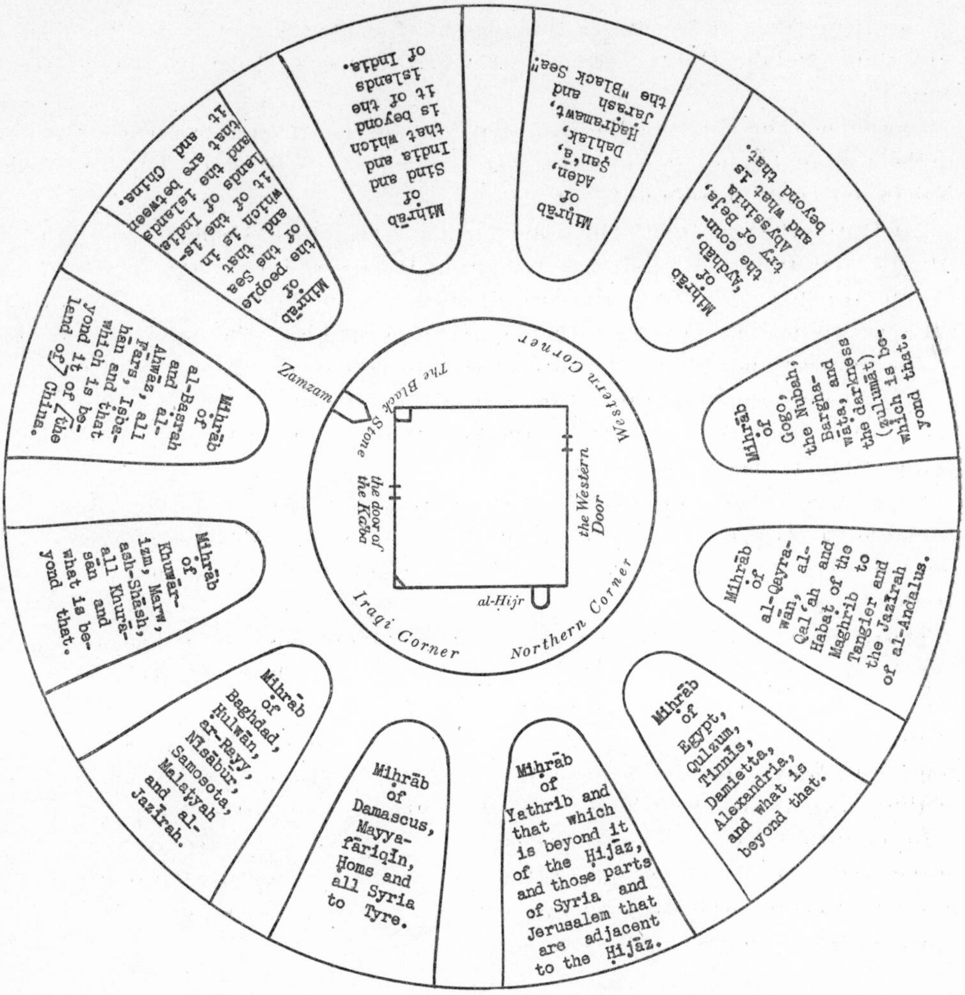

Fig. 5.

Note: Under the Miḥrāb of the People of the Sea, the word *jazāʾir* (islands) incorrectly appears as *ḥaras*. Under the Miḥrāb of Gogo, the Arabic name-form Jojo appears incorrectly as Joḥar; similarly, Barghawāṭah incorrectly appears as Raghūṭah.

Madyan, the island of Cyprus, Alexandria, Constantinople, ʿUmān, al-Rayy, and Farghānah. It also has a share in Harāt and Sijistān.

Gemini has Jurjān, Jīlān, Armenia, Muqān, Miṣr (Cairo), Barqah (Cyrenaica), and Burjabān. It also shares in Iṣbahān and Kirmān.

Cancer has Armenia Minor, eastern Khurāsān, a portion of Tunisia, Hajar, al-Baḥrayn, Daybul, and Marv ar-Rūdh. It has a share in Adharbayjān and Balkh.

Leo has the territory of the Turks, all the way to the land of Gog and Magog and beyond to the end of the oecumene. It also has Ascalon, Jerusalem, Naṣībīn, Melitene, Maysān, Makrān, the land of the Daylam, Īrānshahr, Ṭūs, Upper Egypt, and Tirmidh.

Virgo has Spain, the island of Crete, the capital of Abyssinia, the territory of the Jarāmiqah, Syria, the Euphrates, al-Jazīrah, Diyārbakr, Ṣan'ā', al-Kūfah, and that part of Persia between Kirmān and Sijistān which extends to the borders of Sind.

Libra has the Byzantine Empire and all that which is within its borders, as far as Ifrīqīyah and Sijistān, Kābul, Kashmīr, Upper Egypt to the borders of Abyssinia, Balkh, Harāt, Antioch, Ṭarsūs, Mecca, aṭ-Ṭalaqān, Ṭukhāristān, and China.

Scorpio has the Ḥijāz, al-Madīnah, the Arabian desert, and its various districts to the Yaman, Qūmis, ar-Rayy, Tangier, the land of the Khazars, Āmul, Sāriyah, Nahāwand, and an-Nahrawān. It also has a share in Sogdiana.

Sagittarius has al-Jibāl, Dīnawar, Iṣbahān, Baghdad, Dunbāwand, Bāb al-Abwāb, and Jundi Sābūr. It has a share in Bukhāra, Jurjān, the shores of the Sea of Armenia, and the land of the Berbers to the Maghrib.

Capricorn has Makrān, Sind, the River Mihrān (Indus), the middle of the Sea of 'Umān, to India, China, the eastern Byzantine lands, al-Ahwāz, and Iṣṭakhr.

Aquarius has the Sawād to the district of al-Jīl (Gīlān), al-Kūfah and its countryside, the highlands of the Ḥijāz, the land of the Copts in Egypt, and the land of the Sind. It has a share in Fārs.

Pisces has Ṭabaristān, the northern part of the land of Jurjān, Bukhāra, Samarqand, Qālīqalā, thence to Syria, al-Jazīrah, Cairo, Alexandria, the Sea of the Yaman, and the eastern part of the land of India. It also shares in the territory of the Byzantines.[1]

Thus I found this description in certain *zījs*. It includes repetition of various expressions signifying the same thing in several places. For example, the writer says, "Babylon, Iraq, the Sawād, Baghdad, Nahrawān, al-Kūfah," whereas all of these are of the Sawād, of the land of Babylon, and of Iraq; and Baghdad, Nahrawān, and al-Kūfah are included therein. The foregoing is but an example of this practice. And God knows best the truth of this matter.

In the fifth diagram opposite this page [here on p. 51] is a drawing of the surface of the earth, the plan of the Sacred House (*al-Bayt al-Ḥarām*) and the approximate position of people who turn towards it from all points of the compass. But this is a matter which bears further consideration.

[1] The entire section entitled "On Cities Belonging to Each of the Twelve Signs of the Zodiac" is reproduced from al-Bīrūni, *Tafhīm*, p. 220, where it appears in the form of a table.

CHAPTER THREE

ON THE INTERPRETATION OF TERMS MENTIONED REPEATEDLY IN THIS BOOK

IF WE were to interpret these terms wherever they occur, we should be guilty of undue repetition. Likewise, if we were to mention them in one place but not in another, we should be doing an injustice to one or the other, thus rendering the location thereof ambiguous to the student. On the other hand, if we were to dispense with them entirely, we should put the reader of this book in need of another. We have therefore brought them together, explaining, clarifying and simplifying for the reader the significations thereof.

These terms are: *barīd, farsakh, mīl, kūrah, iqlīm, mikhlāf, istān, ṭussūj, jund, sikkah, miṣr, ābādh, ṭūl, ʿarḍ, darajah, daqīqah, ṣulḥ, silm, ʿanwah, kharāj, fay', ghanīmah,* and *qaṭīʿah.* [1]

Barīd

As regards *barīd,* there is disagreement concerning it. Certain people have maintained that in the desert it is twelve miles, while in Syria and Khurāsān it is six miles. Abu Manṣūr [al-Azhari] [2] has said, "The *barīd* is the *rasūl* (messenger), hence "*ibrāduhu* means *irsāluhu*" [i.e., causing him or it to be despatched]. A certain Arab has said, "Fever is the *barīd* of death," in other words, it is the messenger of death that gives warning thereof. The journey during which prayers may be shortened is four *barīds,* which amounts to forty-eight Hashimite miles such as are used on the road to Mecca. The post-mule (*dābbat al-barīd*) has been called *barīd* because it traverses [3] the distance known as *barīd*. The poet has said:

> And I mount the camel high until I am
> Upon it in the middle of the desert like *barīd.*

Ibn al-Aʿrābi [4] has said, "All that which is between two stations (*manzilayn*) is a *barīd.*"

A certain writer has maintained that which is at variance with the views of those mentioned above. He said:

> From Baghdad to Mecca there are 275 *farsakhs* and two miles, which computed in miles amounts to 827 miles, which comes to 58 *barīds* and four miles. Some *barīds* are 20 miles.

[1] Three other technical terms, namely *rustāq, ṣadaqah* and *khums,* are also discussed in this chapter. Apparently due to an oversight, these terms have been omitted from the above list.

[2] Muḥammad ibn Aḥmad ibn Azhar. Philologist and jurist, A.H. 282/A.D. 895 - A.H. 370/A.D. 980. See *G.A.L.*, I, 129 and *G.A.L. Supplement,* I, 197.

[3] The Arabic equivalent of the English phrase "because it traverses" is erroneously given as *li-sayrihi* in the German edition; it should be *li-sayriha,* as in the Egyptian edition.

[4] Abu ʿAbd Allāh Muḥammad ibn Ziyād. Philologist, geneologist, and transmitter of poetry. Died *ca.* A.H. 231/A.D. 844, aged 81. See *G.A.L.*, I, 117 and *G.A.L. Supplement,* I, 179.

This is an account of his statement. But God is the most knowing.

I have been informed by one who, though unreliable, is nonetheless of sound reasoning and judgment, that the post-horses (*khayl al-barīd*) were called by this name because messengers from certain parts of the realm of a King of the Persians were delayed on their way to him. When they finally came before the King, he inquired of them as to the reason for their tardiness. The messengers complained of the governors they had passed along the way and of their failure to assist them. Whereupon the King caused the governors to be brought into his presence in order to punish them. But the governors pleaded that they had not known these men to be the King's messengers. Thereupon the King commanded that the tails and the manes of the messengers' horses be bobbed as a sign for those they passed, so that they would remove any obstacles which might hinder their progress. Thus people came to say [in Persian] *burīd*, that is to say, bobbed. This word was later arabicized, hence the expression *khayl al-barīd* [1] (post-horses). And God is the most knowing.

Farsakh

As regards the *farsakh*, [2] there has been disagreement concerning it also. Some people have maintained that it is an arabicized Persian word, the origin thereof being *farsank*. Those learned in the language have said that *farsakh* is a pure Arabic word; hence it is said, "I waited for you a *farsakh* of the day," in other words, a long time. Al-Azhari has said, "I believe it is from this that *farsakh* has been derived." Thaʿlab [3] has related after Ibn al-Aʿrābi, saying:

> The *farsakh* has been so called because when a person walks that distance, he sits down and rests.

I say, this is what Thaʿlab said; however, it is a meaningless statement. But God is the most knowing.

It has been related in a tradition transmitted by Ḥudhayfah: [4]

> Between you and the pouring of evil upon you there are many *farsakhs*, except in the event of a certain man's death. For if they say he has died, then evil will be poured upon you in *farsakhs*. [5]

Ibn Shumayl [6] has said in his *Tafsīr* (*Commentary*), "Everything that is abundant

[1] The same definition and etymology are found in al-Khwārizmi, *Mafātīḥ al-ʿUlūm*, p. 63. Most Arabic dictionaries give a similar explanation of the origin of the word *barīd*. According to Hartmann, it is a loan word from the Latin *veredus*. It originally signified post-animal or post-horse, later a courier, and finally the distance between two post-stations, which in Persia was two *farsakhs*, and in other Muslim lands, four *farsakhs*. See article "Barīd" by H. Hartmann in *E. I.*

[2] See article "Farsakh" by Cl. Huart in *E. I.*

[3] Abu al-ʿAbbas Aḥmad ibn Yaḥya ibn Zayd ibn Sayyār. Grammarian and philologist, A.H. 200/A.D. 815 - A.H. 291/A.D. 904. See article "Thaʿlab" by R. Paret in *E.I.*

[4] A. Companion of the Prophet, died A.H. 36. His real name was Ḥusayl ibn Jābir. See Ibn Saʿd, *Kitāb aṭ-Ṭabaqāt*, VI, 8; ʿAbd Allāh ibn Muslim ibn Qutaybah, *Kitāb al-Maʿārif*, ed. F. Wüstenfeld, (Göttingen, 1850), pp. 134-135; and an-Nawawi, *Tahdhīb al-Asmā*ʾ, pp. 199-201.

[5] The man referred to in this *ḥadīth* is said to be ʿUmar ibn al-Khaṭṭāb. This *ḥadīth* is found in Ibn al-Athīr, *an-Nihāyah*, III, 192; az-Zamakhshari, *Kitāb al-Fāʾiq fi Gharīb al-Ḥadīth*, (Ḥaydarābād, A.H. 1324), II, 133-134, and Ibn Manḍūr, *Lisān al-ʿArab*, under "farsakh". A variant of this *ḥadīth* is given in Ibn Saʿd, *Kitāb aṭ-Ṭabaqāt*, III, Part I, 271 and in "Anmerkungen," *ibid.*, p. 49.

[6] An-Naḍr ibn Shumayl. Grammarian and philologist, died A.H. 203/A.D. 818. See *G.A.L.*, I, 102, and *G.A.L. Supplement*, I, 161.

and lasting is *farsakh*." I say, I believe that *farsakh* was derived from this, for a walker finds the *farsakh* too prolonged and endless. In my opinion, Ḥudhayfah's tradition may be taken to mean that evil is poured upon you for a duration of time equal to the length of many *farsakhs*. This does not mean the actual [physical] length of the *farsakh*, but rather the [temporal] magnitude of the length of the *farsakh*, which term is employed to denote a certain distance. But God is the most knowing.

The Kilābīyah have said, "The *farsakhs* of night and day are the hours and the times thereof." Perhaps the *farsakh* is derived from the first signification [i.e. hours]. If this be the origin of the term, the *farsakh* then [as a unit of distance] is derived therefrom. It is as though it were intended to mean a walking distance of an hour or several hours. This would be so if we assume the word to be Arabic.

As regards the extent and meaning of the *farsakh*, there is no choice but to offer an explanation by which both its meaning and that of the mile will be established.

The learned have said that the circumference of the earth at the equator is 360 degrees, that the degree is 25 *farsakhs*, that the *farsakh* is three miles, and that the mile is 4,000 cubits. The *farsakh* then is 12,000 cubits, the cubit being 24 fingers, and the finger being six barleycorns laid side by side. It has been said that the *farsakh* is 12,000 *mursalah* cubits, which are equal to 9,600 *masāḥah* cubits—the *masāḥah* cubit being the same as the Hashimite cubit, which is one and one-fourth *mursalah* cubits. Certain people have said that the *farsakh* amounts to 7,000 paces. However, I have not come upon any difference of opinion concerning the fact that the *farsakh* is three miles. [1]

The Mīl

As regards the *mīl* [2] (mile), Ptolemy in *The Almagest* has said that it amounts to 3,000 King's cubits (*dhirāʿ al-malik*), the cubit being three spans, the span being 36 fingers, and the finger being five barleycorns laid side by side. He also said that the mile is one-third of a *farsakh*. It has been said that the mile is 2,333 paces. As regards lexicologists, the mile according to them represents the extent of vision and its limit. Ibn as-Sikkīt [3] has said:

> The markers along the road to Mecca have been called *amyāl* [milestones], because they were spaced according to the range of vision from one milestone (*mīl*) to another. Now by the range of vision, we do not mean everything that is seen, [4] for we see a mountain from a walking distance of several days. We rather mean the ability of a person of sound vision to see that which is the size

[1] On units of linear measurement used by the Arabs, including *farsakh*, *mīl*, cubit, digits, etc., see Nallino, "Il valore metrico," *Raccolta*, V, 435-452. Nallino cites the above passage and points out that this is another instance where the value of a degree is given as 75 miles. *Ibid.*, 420.

[2] The word *mīl* came to the Arabs by way of Syria and Byzantium, according to Alexander von Humboldt. It appears that the Western Roman *mille passuum* was borrowed by the Byzantines under the form of *mēlion* or *milion*; it then went through the Syriac form of *mīl* or *mīlā* and later passed into the language of the Arabs, who gave it a different value and applied it to an old measure of distance. See *ibid*, 412, where the above passage of Yāqūt's text is discussed.

[3] Abu Yūsuf Yaʿqūb ibn Isḥāq. Philologist and grammarian, died *ca.* A.H. 244/A.D. 858. See article "Ibn al-Sikkīt" by Moh. Ben Cheneb in *E. I.*

[4] This word, which is transcribed erroneously as *marʾan* in the Egyptian edition, should be restored to *marʾīyun* as in the German edition.

of a milestone, which is a structure ten cubits high or thereabouts, its thickness being proportionate to its length.

This, in my opinion, is the best that has been said in this respect.

Iqlīm

As regards the *iqlīm* (clime), its derivation, its limits, and the controversy concerning it have been discussed in Chapter II, which makes it unnecessary to discuss it again. We have listed it herein, however, because it is appropriate that it be here. Since this subject has already been discussed fully in the preceding chapter, we are merely indicating here the place wherein it may be sought.

Kūrah

As regards *kūrah,* [1] Ḥamzah al-Iṣbahāni has mentioned that it is a pure [2] Persian word,—applied to a part of the *istān,*—which the Arabs borrowed, using it to denote the entire *istān,* just as they borrowed *iqlīm* from the Greeks and made it a name for the *kashkhar*. Thus *kūrah* and *istān* are one and the same.

I say, a *kūrah* is any district (*ṣuqʿ*), embracing a number of villages, which must of necessity have a chief town (*qaṣabah*), a city or a river that lends its name to the entire area. Such is the origin of the nomenclature of the *kūrah.* Thus it is said that Dārābjird is a city in Fārs that has a large outlying district (*ʿamal*), the whole outlying district being known as the *kūrah* of Dārābjird. Likewise, Nahr al-Malik is a great river that issues from the Euphrates and flows into the Tigris, and upon it are about 300 villages, the whole area being known as Nahr al-Malik. And such is all that which is similar thereto.

Mikhlāf

As regards *mikhlāf,* [3] it occurs mostly in the speech of the people of the Yaman. It also may occur in the speech of others by way of emulation and imitation. *Mikhlāf* is the singular form of *makhālīf,* which are the *kūrahs* of the Yaman. Each *mikhlāf* is known by a certain name, the name of one of the tribes of the Yaman which settled and cultivated it, and by which name it came to be known. In a *ḥadīth* related by Muʿādh [ibn Jabal] [4] it is stated:

> The *ʿushr* (tithe) and *ṣadaqah* (alms) of him who moves from one *mikhlāf* to another is due to the *mikhlāf* of his tribe when a year has elapsed. [5]

Abu ʿAmr al-Awzāʿi [6] has stated:

> It is said, 'So and so was appointed to administer the *mikhlāfs* of aṭ-Ṭā'if and the outlying areas and districts.'

Khālid ibn Janbah has said:

> In every country there is a *mikhlāf*; in Mecca there is a *mikhlāf,* in al-Madīnah, al-Baṣrah, and al-Kūfah.

[1] See Lane's *Lexicon,* under "*kūrah.*"

[2] In the Egyptian edition, *baḥt,* in the German edition, *maḥt,* both of which are correct.

[3] See Lane's *Lexicon,* under "mikhlāf."

[4] A Companion who was sent by the Prophet as his representative to the Yaman. Died A.H. 18, aged 38 or, according to others, aged 33. See Ibn Saʿd, *Kitāb aṭ-Ṭabaqāt,* III, Part II, 120-126, and Ibn Qutaybah, *Kitāb al-Maʿārif,* p. 135.

[5] This *ḥadīth* is found in Ibn al-Athīr, *an-Nihāyah,* I, 316.

[6] ʿAbd ar-Raḥmān ibn ʿAmr, A.H. 88/A.D. 707 - A.H. 157/A.D. 774. Founder of a school of jurisprudence which disappeared at an early date. See article "al-Awzāʿi" by A. J. Wensinck in *E. I.*

I say that this is a result of practice and custom, as we have already pointed out. For when a Yamāni moves to these areas, he calls the *kūrah* by that name to which he has been accustomed in the speech of his people, whereas in reality *mikhlāf* is but a term peculiar to the language of the people of the Yaman.

Some have said that the *mikhlāf* of a country is its government (*sulṭān*). A certain Arab has been quoted as saying:

> We used to meet the Banu Numayr while we were in the *mikhlāf* of al-Madīnah, and they were in the *mikhlāf* of al-Yamāmah.

Abu Muʿādh has said:

> The *mikhlāf* is the same as the *bunkurd*, [1] which signifies that each group of people administers its alms separately. This is the group's *bunkurd*, which remits alms to the tribe—the same tribe to which such remittance used to be made in the past.

It is stated in *Kitāb al-ʿAyn*: [2]

> They say such a one is from such and such a *mikhlāf*. Among the people of the Yaman it is like the *rustāq*; the plural theorof is *makhālīf*.

I say, these are the accounts that have reached me concerning it. While I have not heard anything concerning the etymology of the word *mikhlāf*, I have a theory regarding it which I now shall state:

When the descendents of Qaḥtān took the land of the Yaman as their dwelling place, wherein they multiplied, they were unable to remain together in one locality. Thereupon they resolved to journey through the various parts of the Yaman, with a view to having each group descended from one father choose a place to occupy and cultivate. Thus whenever the tribes arrived at a particular district and a certain group among them chose it, that group was wont to remain behind therein (*takhallafa bihā*) while the other tribes moved on, the district being named after the father of the tribe that remained behind therein (*al-qabīlah al-mutakhallifah fīhi*). Hence each of these settlements was called a *mikhlāf* because of the practice among these tribes of detaching themselves from the main tribal group and staying behind. Do you not perceive that they have called each of these settlements the *mikhlāf* of Zabīd, the *mikhlāf* of Sanḥān, and the *mikhlāf* of Ḥamdān, which fact indicates that they must have been named after a tribe. But God is the most knowing.

Istān

As regards the *istān*, [3] we have already quoted Ḥamzah al-Iṣbahāni as saying, "The *istān* and the *kūrah* are one and the same." He goes on to say, "Shahrstān, Ṭabarstān and Khūzstān are formed from *istān*, the *alif* [i.e., the "i"] being omitted for the sake of softness."

Fārs comprises five *istāns*, one of which is the *istān* of Dārābjird. The *istān*,

[1] This obviously is a Persian compound noun. It may have been formed from *bun* (origin, root) and *kird* < *gird* (town, locality), i.e., town of origin; or it may have been formed from *baun* (share, portion) and *kird* < *gird*, i.e., town's share or town's fund.

[2] This is in reference to the well-known book by the Arab grammarian and philologist, al-Khalīl ibn Aḥmad (died A.H. 170-75/A.D. 786-91). This book is now lost. See article "al-Khalīl" by Moh. Ben Cheneb in *E. I.*

[3] See Le Strange, *Lands of the Eastern Caliphate*, p. 79, and article "Tasūdj" by V. Minorsky in *E. I.*

in turn, is divided into *rustāqs*, the *rustāq* into *ṭussūjs*, and the *ṭussūj* into a number of villages. For example, Iṣṭakhr (Persepolis) is one of the *istāns* of Fārs, Yazd is one of the *rustāqs* of Iṣṭakhr, Nā'īn and the neighboring villages are one of the *ṭussūjs* of the *rustāq* of Yazd, and Nayāstānah is one of the villages of the *ṭussūj* of Nā'īn.

Mu'ayyad of Rayy has alleged that the meaning of *istān* is "refuge", consequently the Persians say "*istān girift*," in a figurative manner, when a person finds a place wherein he takes refuge.

Rustāq

As regards *rustāq*, [1] according to Ḥamzah ibn al-Ḥasan al-Iṣbahāni, it is derived from *rūdhā festā*. *Rūdhā* is a word signifying a line, a rank, or a row, while *festā* is a noun denoting condition, the signification thereof being: laid out in rows and ordered.

I say, that which we have known and witnessed in our time in the land of the Persians is that by *rustāq* they mean every place wherein there are farms and villages. This term is not applied to cities such as al-Baṣrah and Baghdad, for it is among the Persians as the Sawād is among the people of Baghdad. It has a narrower significance than *kūrah* and *istān*.

Ṭussūj

As regards *ṭussūj* [2] of the measure of *subbūḥ* and *quddūs*, it is a unit that is more specific and smaller than the *kūrah*, the *rustāq*, or the *istān*. It is a part of the *kūrah*, just as the *ṭussūj* is one twenty-fourth part of the *dinār*, for the *kūrah* may include a number of *ṭussūjs*. It is a Persian word derived from "tasu," which word was arabicized by changing the letter "t" to "ṭ" and adding the letter "j" at the end. It was arabicized further by forming its plural as *ṭasāsīj*. This term is employed mainly in the Sawād of Iraq, which has been divided into sixty *ṭussūjs*, each *ṭussūj* being called by a certain name. These *ṭussūjs* have been mentioned in their proper places in our book, the term *ṭussūj* being dropped.

Jund

As regards *jund*, [3] it occurs in such phrases as:

> The *jund* of Qinnasrīn, the *jund* of Filasṭīn, the *jund* of Ḥimṣ, the *jund* of Dimashq, and the *jund* of al-Urdunn.

There are five *junds*, all of which are in Syria, and I have not heard this term used anywhere except in the land of Syria. Al-Farazdaq [4] has said:

Naught, quoth I, save journeying to ash-Shām avails.
For death, like quenchless thirst-sickness, [5] throughout its *junds* prevails. [6]

[1] See Lane's *Lexicon*, under "rustāq."
[2] See article "Tasūdj" by V. Minorsky in *E. I.*
[3] See article "Djund" by Cl. Huart in *E. I.*
[4] Early Muslim poet, A.H. 20/A.D. 640-41 - A.H. 114/A.D. 732-33. His real name was Hammām ibn Ghālib ibn Ṣa'ṣa'ah. See article "al-Farazdaḳ" by A. Schaade in *E. I.*
[5] *Baghar*, rendered here as quenchless thirst-sickness, is said to be a certain kind of malady that afflicts camels. It is characterized by an irresistible craving for water which cannot be satisfied and which eventually causes death. See entry "baghar" in al-Jawhari, *Ṣiḥāḥ*, and Ibn Manḍūr, *Lisān al-'Arab*.
[6] This verse is from a poem in praise of the Umayyad caliph 'Umar ibn 'Abd al-'Azīz. See *Sharḥ Dīwān al-Farazdaq*, ed. 'Abd Allāh Ismā'īl aṣ-Ṣāwi, (Cairo, 1938), p. 220. For a

Aḥmad ibn Yaḥya ibn Jābir al-Balādhuri [1] has said:

> They have disagreed on the meaning of *jund*. Some have said that the Muslims called every one of the *junds* of Syria by that term because each comprised a number of *kūrahs*. The word *tajannud* in this sense signifies "assembling," and the phrase "*jannadtu jundan*" means "I assembled an assembly." [2]

It has also been said:

> The Muslims assigned a *jund* (army) to every district, which came to be known by the name of the army stationed therein and drawing its pay therefrom.
> Thus peope used to say, 'These are the *jund* (troops) of such and such a district,' until in time the name came to denote the army unit as well as the district.

Ābādh

As regards *ābādh*, [3] it occurs frequently in the names of towns, villages, and *rustāqs* mentioned in this book, such as Asadābādh, Rustumābādh, and Ḥuṣnābādh. For example, Asad is the name of a man, while *ābādh* is a Persian word meaning town. Thus the name Asadābādh signifies Asad's town. All such place names are formed in this manner, and they are very numerous.

Sikkah

As regards *sikkah*, it is the traveled [4] road over which caravans pass from one town to another. Thus when it is said in books, "From such a town to such a town there is such and such a *sikkah*," by that is simply meant a road. For example, when it is said, "From Baghdad to Mosul there are five *sikkahs*," this means that a traveler going from Baghdad to Mosul may reach his destination by any one of five roads.

It has been related that by the expression "*sikak al-barīd*" (post-routes), some people mean "*manāzil al-barīd*" (post-stages) where stops are made every day. The first expression is clearer and more correct. But God is the most knowing.

Miṣr

As regards *miṣr* (boundary), it occurs in the statement, "Such and such a ctiy was laid out (*muṣṣirat*) in the time of so and so," [5] or in the statement, "Such and such a city is one of the great cities (*miṣrun min al-amṣār*). *Miṣr* originally signified the limit between two things. The people of Hajar write in their contracts, "Such a one bought from such a one this house with its boundaries (*bi-muṣūrihā*)," in other words with its limits (*bi-ḥudūdihā*).

ʿAdi ibn Zayd [6] has said:

> He who hath made the sun a clear boundary
> That doth set apart the day and the night. [7]

French rendition of this verse see *Divan de Ferazdak*: *Recits de Mohammad-Ben-Habib d'après ibn al-Arabi*, trans. R. Boucher, (Paris, 1870), p. 36.

1 Historian, died A.H. 278/A.D. 892. See article "al-Balādhurī" by C. H. Becker in *E. I.*

2 Cf. al-Balādhuri, *Kitāb Futūḥ al-Buldān*, trans. P. K. Hitti, (New York, 1916), p. 202. See also Yāqūt, *Muʿjam*, I, 136.

3 See article "Ābād" by Cl. Huart in *E. I.*

4 In the German edition, *al-maskūkah*; in the Egyptian edition, more correctly *al-maslūkah*.

5 On the founding of Muslim towns and army camps, see Else Reitemeyer, *Die Städtegründungen der Araber im Islām*: *nach den arabischen Historikern und Geographen*, (Munich, 1912). See also article "Miṣr", section d, by A. J. Wensinck in *E. I.*

6 Pre-Islamic Christian poet, died *ca.* A.D. 604. See R. A. Nicholson, *A Literary History of the Arabs*, (Cambridge, 1953), pp. 40-45, and article "ʿAdī B. Zaid" by A. Haffner in E. I.

7 The passage referring to the people of Hajar and their contract, as well as the verse of

Ṭūl

As regards *ṭūl* (longitude), it occurs in our saying, "The *'arḍ* (latitude) of a town is such and such, and the *ṭūl* (longitude) thereof is such and such." This is a term of the astronomers, which they have explained as follows:

> The signification of the expression, 'its longitude,' is its distance from the extremity of the habitable region, whether calculated on the equinoctial or the equator, or on a circle parallel thereto. This is so because of a similarity among them that makes it possible to substitute one for the other. Because the practice of this science has been derived from the ideas of the Greeks, who reckoned the oecumene (*al-ma'mūrah*) from its extremity that is nearest to them, which is the western extremity, consequently the longitude of a town is calculated on the basis of its distance from the west. There is disagreement among the astronomers, however, regarding this extremity. Some of them calculate longitude from the coast of the Western Ocean, which is the Encircling Sea, while others calculate it from the islands that lie far out in the Western Ocean, some 200 *farsakhs* from the coast. These islands are known as the Fortunate Islands (Jazā'ir as-Sa'ādāt) and the Eternal Islands (al-Jazā'ir al-Khālidāt), and they are off the coast of the country of the Maghrib. For this reason there may be found in the books two sets of longitude, with a difference of ten degrees, for the same town. Intelligence and skill are required in order to distinguish one from the other.[1]

All this is from Abu ar-Rayḥān al-Bīrūni.

'Arḍ

As regards *'arḍ* (latitude), the latitude of a town is the counterpart of its longitude, which has been mentioned before. According to the astronomers:

> It is its farthest distance from the equator in a northerly direction, because all countries and towns are located in this direction. Facing it in the heavens is a great arc, similar to it and located between the zenith and the equinoctial. The elevation of the north pole is equal thereto, and consequently it is used instead of it. The depression of the south pole, even though it is equal to it also, is concealed and we are not aware of it.[2]

These are the words of the author of the *Tafhīm*.

Darajah and Daqīqah

As regards *darajah* (degree)[3] and *daqīqah* (minute), these also are terms employed by the astronomers. They occur in this book in connection with determining longitude and latitude. The astronomers have said that a degree represents the distance of the celestial sphere traversed by the sun in one day and one night, a distance of 25 *farsakhs* in terrestrial terms. The degree is divided into 60 minutes, the minute into 60 seconds, the second into 60 thirds, and so on.

'Adi ibn Zayd, is found in Ibn al-Faqīh, *B.G.A.*, V, 57, where it is attributed to Ibn as-Sikkīt. The same passage is also found in al-Maqrīzi, *al-Mawā'iẓ w-al-I'tibār fi Dhikr al-Khiṭaṭ w-al-Āthār,* (Cairo, A.H. 1270), I, 23, where the source is given as Ibn Qutaybah's *Gharīb al-Ḥadīth.* See also *Tāj al-'Arūs,* under "miṣr."

[1] Al-Bīrūni, *Tafhīm,* pp. 126-127.

[2] *Ibid.,* p. 126.

[3] On the different values assigned to the degree by Arab geographers and astronomers, see Nallino, "Il valore metrico," *Raccolta,* V, 408-457

Ṣulḥ

As regards the term *ṣulḥ* [1] (peace treaty), it occurs in our saying, "Such and such a town was conquered by *ṣulḥ* or by *ʿanwah* (compulsion). The meaning of *ṣulḥ* is derived from *ṣalāḥ* (soundness), which is the opposite of *fasād* (unsoundness). *Ṣulḥ*, as used in this book, is the opposite of *khulf* (disagreement). The meaning of this term may be explained thus: When the Muslims used to march against a fortress or a city the people thereof, being moved by fear, would come out to meet them and arrange to ransom their district by offering *māl* (property), *kharāj* (land-tax), *waẓīfah* (an assessed tax rate) levied each year upon their heads and their lands, or property to be made available to them immediately (*mālan yuʿajjilūnahu lahum*). In other words, such a district cannot be regarded as having been conquered by *ghalabah* (vanquishment), as in the case of *ʿanwah* which signifies vanquishment.

Silm

As regards the term *silm* (peace) in His saying, may He be exalted, "Enter ye into peace, one and all," [2] they have said that by it was meant Islam and its laws. *Silm* means *ṣulḥ*, and *salam* means *istislām* (surrender), or the relinquishment of the reins of power to the will of the Muslims. Thus *silm* appears to be close to *ṣulḥ* in meaning. I am of the opinion that *silm* is derived from *salāmah* (safety). In other words, if the two parties come to terms and arrive at a peaceful settlement, they are then safe from one another. But God is the most knowing.

ʿAnwah

As regards the term *ʿanwah* [3] (compulsion), it occurs in our saying, "Such and such a town was conquered by *ʿanwah*," which is the opposite of *ṣulḥ*. It has been said, "*ʿAnwah* signifies the taking of a thing by vanquishment." It has also been said, "ʿAnwah may be brought about by submission and obedience on the part of those from whom a thing is taken."

Al-Farrā' [4] has recited:

> They took it not by *ʿanwah* out of affection
> But the smiting of the Mashrafi sword yielded it.

They have said, "This usage signifies submission and obedience without fighting." I say, this is a special interpretation of this verse to the effect that *ʿanwah* means obedience. Moreover, it may be so interpreted as to preclude its falling within the meaning of usurpation or vanquishment. Thus it may be said that the meaning of the statement, "They did not take it by vanquishment notwithstanding affection, but fighting caused it to be taken by *ʿanwah*," is like saying, "Zayd did not wrong you out of love, but out of hatred." It is also like saying, "This act did not issue from a pure heart, if there was a pure heart, in other words it issued from an impure heart." This is similar to His saying, may He be exalted:

> The Jews [and the Christians] have said, 'We are the children of God, and His beloved.' Say, why then does he chastise you for your sins? [5]

[1] See article "Dār al-Ṣulḥ" by D. B. Macdonald in *E. I.*
[2] Qur'ān II, 204.
[3] See Lane's *Lexicon*, under "ʿanwah."
[4] Grammarian and philologist, died A.H. 207/A.D. 822. See *G.A.L.*, I, 116, and *G.A.L. Supplement*, I, 178.
[5] Qur'ān V, 21. The phrase "and the Christians" does not appear in either the German or the Egyptian edition of the *Muʿjam*.

It is appropriate to regard the poet's saying, "They took it," as a proof of vanquishment and defeat. Were it not so, he would have said, "They surrendered it not." For if one were to say, "The prince took such and such a fortress," the signification would be that he took it as a result of the enemy's defeat. But if one were to say, "The people of such and such a fortress surrendered it," the signification would be that they submitted willingly and by choice. This is evident.

The consensus is that *ʿanwah* signifies vanquishment. From it is derived the word *ʿāni*, which means captive. It is said, "I took him by *ʿanwah*," in other words, by coercing and defeating him. It is also said, "This city was conquered by *ʿanwah*, in other words, by fighting, whereby its defenders were fought until they were vanquished, or were unable to hold it; whereupon they abandoned it, removing themselves therefrom without concluding a peace treaty with the Muslims.

Kharāj

As regards the term *kharāj* [1] (land-tax), it has the same meaning as *kharj*. A slave pays you his *kharāj* or revenue (*ghallah*). Likewise, subjects (*raʿīyah*) pay *kharāj* to governors. It originates in His saying, may He be exalted, "Dost thou ask them for remuneration (*kharj*) . . . ?" [2] And *kharj* has been read as *kharāj*. The meaning of the verse is: Would you ask them a remuneration for that which you brought forth? Surely the remuneration and the reward of you Lord are better.

As regards the *kharāj* which ʿUmar ibn al-Khaṭṭāb imposed upon the Sawād and other *fay*ʾ lands, it signifies revenue. And in the same vein is the Prophet's saying, "*al-kharāj biḍ-ḍamān*" [3] (revenue is contingent upon liability). They have said that this expression pertains to revenue derived from the labors of a slave purchased by a man who, after working him for a time, discovers in him a defect that had been concealed by the seller. He is entitled to return the slave to the seller and to recover the whole price thereof. The revenue derived by the purchaser from the labours of the slave is lawfully his, for the slave had been in his possession, and had he perished, he would have perished as part of his property. [4]

When ʿUmar ibn al-Khaṭṭāb [5] ordered the surveying of the Sawād, he gave it to the farmers thereof to cultivate in return for a certain share of the annual revenue. For this reason it was called *kharāj*. Those countries that were conquered by peace treaty, and upon whose lands were imposed the assessed tax rates required by the peace settlement, later came to be known as *kharāj* lands. This assessed tax rate was similar to the *kharāj* imposed upon the farmers. It is the same as *ghallah* (revenue), for the general meaning of *kharāj* is *ghallah*.

It is related in the *ḥadīth* that when Abu Ṭaybah cupped the Prophet, the

[1] See article "Kharādj" by T. W. Juynboll in *E. I.*

[2] Qurʾān XXIII, 74.

[3] This *ḥadīth* is found in Ibn Ḥanbal, *Musnad*, VI, 49, 208,237; at-Tirmidhi, *Ṣaḥīḥ*, V, 286, and other *ḥadīth* collections. See *C.T.M.*, II, 22.

[4] The above passage bears some resemblance to Ibn Sallām's explanation of this legal concept. See Ibn Sallām, *Kitāb al-Amwāl*, p. 73. An almost identical version of the passage appears in Ibn Manḍūr's *Lisān al-ʿArab*, where it is attributed to Ibn Sallām. This fact suggests the possibility that Yāqūt may have copied it, either from some version of *Kitāb al-Amwāl* other than the one we now possess, or from some other work by Ibn Sallām.

[5] The second orthodox caliph, died A.H. 23/A.D. 644, aged 53. See article "ʿUmar ibn al-Khaṭṭāb" by G. Levi della Vida in *E. I.*

Prophet ordered that he be given two *ṣā'ṣ* of food, and he also spoke to his family and they reduced his *kharāj*, in other words his *ghallah*. [1]

Fay'

As regards the term *fay'* [2], its primary signification is "returning". [3] Likewise, there is the *fay'* (umbra) that comes in the evening, following the *ẓill* (shade or shadow) cast by trees and other objects in the morning. Thus Ḥumayd ibn Thawr [4] has said:

> "Neither can we bear the *ẓill*, due to the early morning's cold,
> Nor can we enjoy the *fay'*, due to the cold of the evening." [5]

Abu ʿUbaydah [6] has said:

> Whatever the sun shines upon and withdraws from constitutes both *fay'* and *ẓill*, but that upon which the sun shines not is only *ẓill*. [7]

Another instance of this usage is His saying, may He be exalted, on *ahl al-baghy* [8] (the impious and the unjust), ". . . until they revert (*tafi'a*) to the precepts of God, etc.", [9] in other words, until they return (*tarjiʿu*) etc.

Thus property [taken from the enemy] has been called *fay'* because it reverted to the Muslims from the possessions of the infidels.

Abu Manṣūr al-Azhari has maintained, regarding His saying, may He be exalted, "That which God has restored (*afā'a*) to His Apostle from the people of the villages, etc.": [10]

[1] The text of this *ḥadīth* closely follows the version given in at-Tirmidhi, *Ṣaḥīḥ*, V, 278. The same *ḥadīth* is found in most *ḥadīth* collections. See *C. T. M.*, I, 428. See also Ibn Saʿd, *Kitāb aṭ-Ṭabaqāt*, Vol. I, Part II, 143.

[2] See article "Fai'" by T. W. Juynboll in *E. I.*

[3] It should be pointed out that this term has been variously rendered as "returning", "reverting," or "restoring," depending on the context.

[4] Early Muslim poet and Companion. He is said to have eulogized the Prophet in a poem and to have been converted to Islam by him. The above verse quoted by Yāqūt is from a love poem addressed to a tree. Ḥumayd ibn Thawr seems to have resorted to allegory after ʿUmar ibn Khaṭṭāb had forbidden poets to address amorous poems to women. See Ibn Ḥajar al-ʿAsqalāni, *Kitāb al-Iṣābah fi Tamyīz aṣ-Ṣaḥābah*, (Cairo, A.H. 1323), I, 39-40; and Abu al-Faraj al-Iṣbahāni, *al-Aghāni*, (Cairo, A.H. 1285), IV, 98.

[5] In both the German and Egyptian editions the word *nastaṭīʿuhu* (can we bear it) is erroneously given as *tastaṭīʿuhu* (can she bear it), probably due to a misreading of diacritical marks. The same error resulted in the substitution of *tadhūqu* (can she enjoy) for *nadhūqu* (can we enjoy). This misreading seems to have been widespread long before Yāqūt's time. The grammarian Abu al-ʿAbbās Thaʿlab (d. A.H. 291) quotes this poem and states that the first letters of the two words in question should be read as *nūn* instead of *tā'*. See Thaʿlab, *Kitāb Faṣīḥ al-Lughah al-ʿArabīyah*, with an interpretation by Abu Sahl Muḥammad ibn ʿAli ibn Muḥammad al-Harawi, entitled *at-Talwīḥ fi Sharḥ al-Faṣīḥ*, (Cairo, A.H. 1325/A.D. 1907), p. 90. Yāqūt reproduces this same verse, together with the rest of the poem, later in his text under the entry "al-Abṭaḥ." (See Vol. I, p. 93 of the German edition, where it appears in its correct form, and Vol I, p. 85 of the Egyptian edition, where the error stands uncorrected.) It should be pointed out that this verse is not given correctly in all the sources cited in the preceding footnote.

[6] Maʿmar ibn al-Muthanna at-Taymi. Philologist and geneologist, A.H. 114 - A.H. 208-11. See *G.A.L.*, I, 103, and *G.A.L. Supplement*, I, 47 and 162.

[7] According to Thaʿlab (*Kitāb Faṣīḥ al-Lughah*, p. 90), Abu ʿUbaydah made this statement on the authority of Ru'bah ibn al-ʿAjjāj.

[8] Cf. Abu al-Ḥasan al-Māwardi, *Kitāb al-Aḥkām as-Sulṭānīyah*, ed. M. Enger, (Bonn, 1853), pp. 96-102; Yaʿqūb ibn Ibrāhīm Abu Yūsuf, *Kitāb al-Kharāj*, (Cairo, A.H. 1302), p. 118.

[9] Qur'ān XLIX, 9.

[10] Qur'ān LIX, 7.

In other words, that which God restored to the people of His religion, from the property of those who were opposed to them but who did not resort to fighting. They had either to evacuate their homelands and abandon them to the Muslims, or else conclude a peace settlement providing for *jizyah* (poll-tax) which they were to pay on their heads, or property other than poll-tax which they were to offer as ransom to avert the shedding of their blood. This property is the *fay'* mentioned in the Book of God.

Said God, may He be exalted, 'And that which God has restored to His Apostle, from their spoils, you pursued not by horse or camel (*fa-ma awjaftum*) . . .' [1] In other words, you failed to pursue them with horse or camel.

This verse was inspired in connection with the property of Banu an-Naḍīr when they broke their pledge, leaving their homeland for Syria. Thereupon the Messenger of God divided their property, comprising date palms and other things, in accordance with those purposes for which God wanted it divided. The division of *fay'* differs from the division of *ghanīmah,* which is acquired as a result of pursuit by horse or camel.

I say, this is an account of al-Azhari's view, which is the same as that propounded by the school of the *imām* ash-Shāfiʿi. [2] If *fay'*, as we have stated, signifies "returning," then it matters not whether the spoils are restored to the Muslims as a result of pursuit by horse or camel or by other means. Furthermore, it does not matter whether it be restored to the Messenger of God in particular or to the Muslims in general. As regards the verse in question, it is but an account of the actual circumstances of the story of Banu an-Naḍīr, wherein there is no evidence as to whether or not *fay'* involves pursuit by horse or camel. For these are merely the circumstances of the case. Had this property been restored as a result of pursuit by horse or camel, and had it accrued to the Muslims as a whole, then it would have been possible for the verse to have stated, "That which God hath restored to the faithful from the people of the villages."

However, the restoration of *fay'* to the Messenger of God in the absence of pursuit by horse or camel is sufficient proof that, in the event of such pursuit, it is to be restored to others. Had not both situations been basically the same, the negative statement surely would have been dispensed with. Had the affirmative statement been comprehensible, without that which negates it, God, may He be exalted, would have found it sufficient to have said, "That which God restored to His Messenger from the people of the villages."

And Qudāmah [3] has reversed the statement of al-Azhari by saying:

Fay' is the name given to that part of the enemy's country against which the Muslims have prevailed by coercion, through fighting and war, as a result of which it was assigned to them in perpetuity (*juʿila mawqūfan ʿalayhim*). For that which is collected by taxation therefrom returns to them every year.

I say that Qudāmah's designation of *fay'* property as being only that which has been gained by coercion, through fighting, is erroneous. For that which he has called *fay'* occurs in His saying, may He be exalted, "And that which God

[1] Qur'ān LIX, 6.

[2] Abu ʿAbd Allāh Muḥammad ibn Idrīs, A.H. 150/A.D. 767 - A.H. 204/A.D. 820. Founder of the Shāfiʿi school of law. See article "al-Shāfiʿī" by W. Heffening in *E.I.*

[3] Abu al-Faraj al-Kātib al-Baghdādi. Man of letters and Abbasid administrator, died A.H. 337/A.D. 958. The above quotation is probably from his *Kitāb al-Kharāj,* which he is said to have compiled after A.H. 316. Only the second volume of this book survives in the Köprülü library in Istanbul. Extracts from it have been published by de Goeje in *B.G.A.*, VI. See article "Ḳudāma" by C. Brockelmann in *E.I.*

restored to His Apostle from them, etc." Whereas that which is relied upon is that *fay'* is whatever has been settled upon the Muslims and has reverted to them from the unbelievers, whereby it is restored to them every year. This includes the revenues of *kharāj*, *jizyah*, and the property of the Banu an-Naḍīr, Wādi al-Qura, and Fadak, which were conquered by peace and were not pressed upon by horse or camel, as well as the possessions of the Sawād, which were conquered by force and later confirmed in the hands of its people, provided they pay the *kharāj* thereof every year.

There is no disagreement among the learned concerning the fact that what was conquered by peace, such as the property of the Banu an-Naḍīr and others, is called *fay'*; likewise, those parts of the Sawād and other lands which were conquered by force and which were confirmed in the hands of the inhabitants were also called *fay'*. The difference between the two, however, lies in the fact that what was conquered by *'anwah* became *fay'* to the Muslims who participated in its conquest and was divided among them, as the Apostle of God did with regard to the property of Khaybar. This is also called *ghanīmah*. As regards those who desired peace, such as Wādi al-Qura and Fadak, or those who evacuated their homelands without any of the Muslims having marched against them, as in the case of the Banu an-Naḍīr, the decision in this matter is left to the Apostle of God and to the *imāms* who came after him. The *imāms* may divide such property among whomsoever they wish, following the example of the Apostle of God with regard to the property of the Banu an-Naḍīr.

Ghanīmah

As regards *ghanīmah*, [1] it comprises those lands that have been taken as booty from the property of the polytheists, such as the land of Khaybar. For the Prophet divided it among his Companions after deducting one fifth. As a result, every parcel of land passed into the hands of a particular owner. This was not the case with the lands of the Sawād, which were also conquered by force, and which 'Umar decided to assign to the Muslim community as a whole. Thus these lands were not divided, but became *fay'* reverting to the Muslims every year.

Ghanīmah includes *al-amwāl aṣ-ṣāmitah* (silent property), a fifth of which is deducted and the remainder divided among those participating in the fighting, the horseman receiving three shares and the foot soldier one share. [2] This is something I arrived at by the process of analogy, without having seen a provision to this effect.

Later I happened to come upon *Kitāb al-Amwāl* (*The Book of Property*) by Abu 'Ubayd al-Qāsim ibn Sallām. [3] This I found to be in accord with that which I had maintained, and to confirm it, for he said: [4]

[1] See article "Ghanīma" by Th. W. Juynboll in *E.I.*

[2] Cf. ash-Shāfi'i, *Kitāb al-Umm*, (Būlāq, A.H. 1321), VII, 306-307; Abu Yūsuf, *Kitāb al-Kharāj*, p. 11; Abu Ja'far Muḥammad ibn Jarīr aṭ-Ṭabari, *Das Konstantinopler Fragment des Kitāb Iḫtilāf al-Fuqahā'*, ed. Joseph Schacht, (Leyden, 1934), pp. 80-81; Abu Yūsuf, *ar-Radd 'ala Siyar al-Awzā'i*, ed. Abu al-Wafā' al-Afghāni, (Cairo, n.d.), pp. 17-21; and al-Māwardi, *al-Aḥkām as-Sulṭānīyah*, p. 243.

[3] Philologist and jurist, A.H. 154/A.D. 770 - A.H. 223/A.D. 837. See article "Abū 'Ubaid" by C. Brockelmann in *E.I.*

[4] The following quotation is faithfully reproduced from Ibn Sallām's *Kitāb al-Amwāl*, pp. 16-17

The property over which the *imāms* of the Muslims have jurisdiction is of three kinds.

This he deduced from the Book of God.

These are *ṣadaqah* [alms], *fay'*, and *khums* [fifth]. These are general names, each of which includes various kinds of property.

Ṣadaqah: As regards *ṣadaqah*, [1] it is the *zakāh* of the property of Muslims, which includes gold, silver, camels, cattle, sheep, grain and fruits. These are for the eight categories that God has named in the Qur'ān, [2] to which none is entitled save they. 'Umar ibn al-Khaṭṭāb has said, 'The revenue accruing from this property belongs to these categories.' [3]

Fay': As regards *fay'* property, it is that which has been collected from the property of the *dhimmis*, including the *jizyah* of their heads, through which the shedding of their blood was averted and their property made inviolate, in consideration of a certain tax agreed upon by a peace treaty. This also includes the *kharāj* of lands conquered by force which the *imām* has confirmed in the hands of the *dhimmis* in consideration of a *ṭasq* [4] (fixed rate of tax) to be paid every year. Another form of impost is the *waẓīfah* (assessed tax rate) imposed upon those *ṣulḥ* lands whose owners continued to defend them until they were granted a peace treaty in consideration of a specified *kharāj*. There is also that which the *'āshir* (tax collector) levies on the merchandise of the *dhimmis*, which they carry [5] past him in the course of their trade, and that which is levied on the *ḥarbis* when they enter the countries of Islam for commerce.

All these taxes come under *fay'*, which accrues to all Muslims, rich and poor alike. It is disbursed for such purposes as the stipends of soldiers, and the allowances of their offspring, and for such of the affairs of the people as the *imām* attends to, with a view to the well-being of Islam and its adherents.

Khums

As regards *khums*, it comprises one-fifth of the *ghanā'im* (spoils) taken from the *ḥarbis*, and also *ar-rikāz al-'Ādi* [6] (ancient buried treasure) and the *'arḍ* (articles of trade) or metals. But there has been disagreement among men of learning concerning the last two. Some of them have said that the *khums* applies to the five categories mentioned in the Qur'ān, concerning which 'Umar said, "This [revenue] belongs to these categories." [7] Others have said that *khums* is

[1] See article "Ṣadaḳa" by T. H. Weir in *E.I.*

[2] The word *al-aṣnāf* (the categories) in the German edition should be restored to *lil-aṣnāf* (for the categories), as in the Egyptian edition and in Ibn Sallām's text.

[3] According to the Qur'ān, "The *ṣadaqāt* are for the poor, the needy, those engaged in the collection and distribution thereof, those whose hearts are to be conciliated, for the ransoming of slaves, for the debtors, for the cause of God, and for the wayfarer." Qur'ān IX, 60. The decision as to who should be the beneficiaries of *ṣadaqah*, *fay'*, and *khums* property is ascribed to 'Umar ibn al-Khaṭṭāb, who is said to have announced it in the presence of al-'Abbās and 'Ali ibn Abi Ṭālib. See Ibn Sallām, *Kitāb al-Amwāl*, pp. 14-15.

[4] In the Egyptian edition, *qisṭ* (portion, installment) should be restored to *ṭasq* (fixed tax rate), as in the German edition and in Ibn Sallām's text.

[5] In the German edition the word *tamurrūn*, occurring in the phrase *tamurrūn bihā 'alayhi* (you carry it past him) should be restored to *yamurrūn*, so as to read *yamurrūn bihā 'alayhi* (they carry it past him). This phrase appears correctly in the Egyptian edition and in Ibn Sallām's text.

[6] The levying of this tax is based on the *ḥadīth*, "Upon the *rikāz*, one fifth is to be levied." This is found in most *ḥadīth* collections. See *C.T.M.*, II, 83. Cf. al-Māwardi, *al-Aḥkām as-Sulṭānīyah*, p. 207; Ibn Sallām, *Kitāb al-Amwāl*, pp. 336-342 (art. 856-873); Muḥammad ibn al-Ḥasan, *al-Jāmi' aṣ-Ṣaghīr*, printed on the margin of Abu Yūsuf, *Kitāb al-Kharāj*, (Cairo, A.H. 1302), pp. 22-23; and Abu Yūsuf, *Kitāb al-Kharāj*, pp. 12-13.

[7] These five categories are enumerated in the following *sūrah*: "And know ye, that whatever ye take as spoils, to God belongs a fifth thereof, and to the Apostle, and to the near of kin, the orphans, the needy and the wayfarer . . ." Qur'ān VIII, 42.

treated in the same manner as *fay'*, the disposition thereof being left to the discretion of the *imām*. If he decides to grant it to those mentioned by God, he may do so; on the other hand, if he decides that it is best for the Muslims and most advantageous to their welfare, he may deposit it in the public treasury. It is to be held in readiness, in case a calamity should befall them, or in case a matter of public interest, requiring attention, should confront them, such as the defense of a frontier fortress, the provision of weapons and horses, or the payment of the allowances of the beneficiaries of *fay'* such as soldiers, judges, and others like them.

Qaṭīʿah

As regards *qaṭīʿah* [1] (fief), it is of two kinds. First, if the *imām* who exercises legitimate authority and to whom obedience is due decides to set apart a piece of land from that which borders upon it, he may present it as a gift to whomsoever he chooses, to develop it and to derive benefit therefrom. He may turn it into houses to be occupied by him or by whomsoever he wishes, or he may turn it into a farm. In both cases he enjoys whatever revenue accrues from it. While the fief-holder is not subject to the payment of *kharāj*, the tenant farmer cultivating his farm may be made subject to it. This is the present state of the *qaṭīʿahs* (fiefs) of al-Manṣūr and of his descendants after him in Baghdad. These *qaṭīʿahs* include the *qaṭīʿah* of ar-Rabīʿ, the *qaṭīʿah* of Umm Jaʿfar, and so on. All these *qaṭīʿahs* have been mentioned in their proper places in this book.

The other kind of *qaṭīʿah* is said to exist when the *sulṭān* (ruler) grants villages and provinces to whomsoever he wishes from among his army commanders and other officials, imposing upon them an annual tax. The ruler does not ask the person enfeoffed to pay anything more than the specified amount required of him, regardless of whether or not the revenue accruing from the fief diminishes or increases, is abundant or in short supply.

[1] See article "Iḳṭāʿ" by M. Sobernheim in *E.I.*, and Frede Lokkegaard, *Taxation in Early Islam in the Classic Period*, (Copenhagen, 1950), Chapters I and II.

CHAPTER FOUR

ON THE VIEWS OF JURISTS ON LEGAL PROVISIONS GOVERNING *FAY'* AND *GHANĪMAH* LANDS AND THE MANNER OF THEIR DIVISION

MASLAMAH IBN MUḤĀRIB [1] has said:

> Qaḥdham [2] related to me that Ziyād [ibn Abīhi] [3] endeavored, during his governorship, to separate *ṣulḥ* from *'anwah,* but he was unable to do so, despite the proximity of his times to the period of conquests and despite the presence of those who had participated therein.

As regards the legal provision in this matter, [4] it is to withhold one-fifth of the *ghanīmah* [for the public treasury], dividing the remaining four-fifths among the seizers thereof. Certain jurists have said that this is up to the *imām*. If he decides to regard it as *ghanīmah,* withholding one-fifth and distributing the remainder as the Apostle of God did with regard to Khaybar, he may do so. [5] On the other hand, if he decides to regard it as *fay',* he neither divides it into fifths nor distributes it. Instead it is divided among all the Muslims, as 'Umar ibn al-Khaṭṭāb, [6]—on the advice [7] of 'Ali ibn Abi Ṭālib, [8] Mu'ādh ibn Jabal, and other leading Companions,—did with regard to the land of the Sawād, the land of Egypt, and other territories that he conquered by force of arms.

The Apostle of God acted in accordance with His saying, may He be exalted:

> And know ye, that whatever ye take as spoils, to God belongs a fifth thereof, and to the Apostle, and to the near of kin, the orphans, the needy and the wayfarer . . . [9]

[1] Maslamah ibn 'Abd Allāh ibn Sa'īd ibn Muḥārib al-Fihri Abu Muḥārib. Well-known grammarian and tutor to Ja'far, son of Abu Ja'far al-Manṣūr. See as-Suyūṭi, *Bughyat al-Wu'āh,* p. 391.

[2] Prominent figure in the tax administration of Iraq under the Umayyads. He reached the peak of his career (*ca.* A.D. 738) as secretary to the governor of Iraq, Yūsuf ibn 'Umar. Various writers have vocalized his name differently. In the Yāqūt text it appears as Qaḥdham, which is the way it appears in an-Nawawi's *Tahdhīb al-Asmā',* another work edited by Wüstenfeld. Sprengling believes that the name is correctly vocalized as Quḥdhum in Ibn 'Abdūs al-Jahshiyāri, *Kitāb al-Wuzarā' w-al-Kuttāb,* ed. Mžik, (Leipzig, 1926). See Martin Sprengling, "From Persian to Arabic," *A.J.S.L.,* LVI (1939), 175-224, 325-336.

[3] Ziyād "the son of his father." Viceroy of Iraq and the eastern half of the caliphate and half-brother of Mu'āwiyah. Died A.H. 56-57. See article "Ziyād ibn Abīhi" by H. Lammens in *E.I.*

[4] This part of Chapter IV, dealing with the division of conquered lands (from this point up to the middle of page 69), seems to be based upon Ibn Sallām's *Kitāb al-Amwāl.* In order to point out as accurately as possible the various passages from Ibn Sallām incorporated into Yāqūt's text, reference will be made to them by page and line number.

[5] Cf. Ibn Sallām, *Kitāb al-Amwāl,* p. 55_{7-10}.

[6] *Ibid.,* p. 55_{10-12}.

[7] *Ibid.,* p. 60_{8-9}.

[8] The fourth orthodox caliph, cousin and son-in-law of the Prophet. Died A.H. 40/A.D. 661, aged 58 or 63. See article "'Alī ibn Abī Ṭālib" by Cl. Huart in *E. I.*

[9] Qur'ān VIII, 42. Cf. Ibn Sallām, *Kitāb al-Amwāl,* p. 60_{19-20}.

This [1] is what az-Zubayr [2] advised in Egypt, and Bilāl [3] in Syria, and it is the doctrine of Mālik ibn Anas. [4] For, according to them, *ghanīmah* belongs to the seizers thereof, to the exclusion of other people. [5] ʿUmar ibn al-Khaṭṭāb, ʿAli ibn Abi Ṭālib, and Muʿādh ibn Jabal relied [6] upon His saying, might and majesty to Him: [7]

> That which God restored without fighting unto His Apostle from the people of the villages, belongs to God and to the Apostle and to the near of kin, the orphans, the needy, and the wayfarer . . . [8]

until He says, may He be exalted:

> To the poor refugees who were driven from their homes . . . [9] And those who came into the City and into the faith before them. . .[10] And those who came [into the faith] after them . . . [11]

Sufyān ath-Thawri [12] followed this view. [13]

If the *imām* divides the land among its conquerors as the Apostle of God did with regard to the lands of Khaybar, it becomes tithe land (*ʿushrīyah*), and the people thereof become slaves. On the other hand, if he does not divide it but leaves it to the Muslims as a whole, then the *jizyah* is imposed upon the necks of its people, whereby they are freed, while the *kharāj* is imposed upon the land, which remains in the hands of its owners. [14] This is the view of Abu Ḥanīfah. [15]

If a man among those conquered by force embraces Islām and his land is confirmed in his possession, he cultivates it and pays the *kharāj* therefor.[16] There is no disagreement by any group on this matter. He becomes subject to the *kharāj* and is required to pay *zakāh* for the remainder of what the land produces after the deduction of the *kharāj*, provided that the seed amounts to five *wasqs* (camel-loads). [17]

[1] *Ibid.*, p. 60_{4-6}.
[2] Az-Zubayr ibn al-ʿAwwām. Cousin and Companion of Muḥammad and one of the earliest converts to Islam. Died in the Battle of the Camel (*circa* A.D. 656) at the age of 60-67. See article "al-Zubair b. al-ʿAwwām" by A. J. Wensinck in *E.I.*
[3] A slave of Abyssinian origin who became the first muʾadhdhin in Islam. Died A.H. 20/-A.D. 641 or, according to others, A.H. 21-28 at the age of 60. See article "Bilāl" by F. Buhl in *E.I.*
[4] Founder of the Māliki school of law. Died A.H. 179/A.D. 795, aged 85. See article "Mālik ibn Anas" by J. Schacht in *E.I.*
[5] Ibn Sallām, *Kitāb al-Amwāl*, p. 60_{20-21}.
[6] *Ibid.*, p. 61_{9-10}.
[7] The following verses of Sūrah LIX are found in the texts of both Ibn Sallām and Yāqūt. The former quotes verses 7, 8, and 9 in full, and the opening words of 10. See *ibid.*, pp. 60-61. Yāqūt, however, quotes the first half of verse 7 and verse 8, and the opening words of 9 and 10.
[8] Qurʾān LIX, 7.
[9] Qurʾān LIX, 8.
[10] Qurʾān LIX, 9.
[11] Qurʾān LIX, 10.
[12] Traditionist and jurist. Born A.H. 95-97/A.D. 715-716; died A.H. 161-162/A.D. 777-778. See article "Sufyān al-Thawri" by M. Plessner in *E. I.*
[13] Ibn Sallām, *Kitāb al-Amwāl*, p. 60_{20}.
[14] Cf. aṭ-Ṭabari, *Ikhtilāf*, p. 218_{8-9}.
[15] An-Nuʿmān ibn Thābit ibn Zūṭā, A.H. 81/A.D. 700 - A.H. 150/A.D. 767. Founder of the Ḥanafi school. See article "Abū Ḥanīfa" by Th. W. Juynboll and A. J. Wensinck in *E.I.*
[16] Cf. Abu Yūsuf, *Kitāb al-Kharāj*, pp. 35-36; Ibn Sallām, *Kitāb al-Amwāl*, pp. 101, 155; aṭ-Ṭabari, *Ikhtilāf*, pp. 218-219; Yaḥya ibn Ādam, *Kitāb al-Kharāj*, pp. 59-62 (art. 181-194).
[17] This legal principle is traced to the *ḥadīth* of the Prophet: "No *zakāh* is levied on produce amounting to less than five *wasqs*." This *ḥadīth* is found in most *ḥadīth* collections. See *C.T.M.*, II, 338. See also Ibn Sallām, *Kitāb al-Amwāl*, pp. 479-480; Yaḥya ibn Ādam, *Kitāb al-Kharāj*, pp. 135-139 (art. 438-456); Muḥammad ibn al-Ḥasan, *al-Jāmiʿ aṣ-Ṣaghīr*, p. 21; and Abu Yūsuf, *Kitāb al-Kharāj*, pp. 30-31.

It has been related of ʿAli ibn Abi Ṭālib that he said, "Naught save *kharāj* is levied upon *kharāj* land." [1] In other words, he said that a Muslim is not to be burdened by both *kharāj* and *zakāh*. This is the view of Abu Ḥanīfah and his followers. [2] Abu Yūsuf and Sharīk ibn ʿAbd Allāh [3] have said of others:

> When a Muslim rents *kharāj* land, the owner of the land is subject to *kharāj*, while the Muslim is subject to *zakāh* on the land, if the produce thereof amounts to five camel-loads. [4]

Al-Ḥasan [ibn Ṣāliḥ ibn Ḥayy] [5] has held that the landlord is subject to *kharāj*, while the tenant is not subject to anything. [6]

Abu Ḥanīfah and Abu Yūsuf have said that the wages of him who collects the *ʿushr* and the *kharāj* revenues are payable from the total amount of produce measured [before the collection of the tax]. Sufyān was of the opinion that wages paid for collecting land tax (*ujūr al-kharāj*) are to be borne by the owners of the land. Mālik ibn Anas has said that wages paid for collecting *ʿushr* are to be borne by the landowner, while wages paid for collecting *kharāj* are to be equally shared by the government and the landowner. [7]

Mālik, Abu Ḥanīfah, and the majority of the jurists have maintained that if any person among those conquered by force neglects to cultivate his land, he is enjoined to cultivate it and to pay the *kharāj* on it; if he fails to comply, he is ordered to turn it over to someone else. [8] As regards tithe land, he is not subject to these requirements. If he cultivates it, *ṣadaqah* is levied upon it; if he refuses to pay, that is up to him. It has been said that if he constructs buildings comprising shops and the like on tithe land, he is not liable to anything. If he turns it into an orchard, however, he becomes subject to *kharāj*. [9]

Mālik ibn Anas, Ibn Abi Dhi'b, [10] and Abu ʿAmr al-Awzāʿi [11] have said that should the produce be stricken by a natural calamity, its owner is exempted from *kharāj*.[12] According to Abu Ḥanīfah, if a *kharāj* land happens to be owned by a slave, a *mukātab*,[13] or a woman, it is subject only to *kharāj*.[14] On the other hand, Sufyān, Ibn Abi Dhi'b, and Mālik have held that it is subject to *kharāj*, and that the remainder of the produce [after the deduction of *kharāj*] is subject to *ʿushr*.

[1] Cf. Yaḥya ibn Ādam, *Kitāb al-Kharāj*, p. 168 (art. 616).

[2] See al-Māwardi, *al-Aḥkām as-Sulṭānīyah*, p. 238; aṭ-Ṭabari, *Ikhtilāf*, p. 226_{18-19}.

[3] Traditionist and judge, died A.H. 177/A.D. 793-4 or A.H. 178. See Ibn Saʿd, *Kitāb aṭ-Ṭabaqāt*, pp. 263-264; Ibn Khallikān, *Wafayāt*, I, 317-318.

[4] Cf. Yaḥya ibn Ādam, *Kitāb al-Kharāj*, pp. 164-165 (art. 599).

[5] Traditionist, jurist, and a leader of Zaydi Shiʿism, A.H. 100 - A.H. 168. See Ibn an-Nadīm, *al-Fihrist*, I, 178.

[6] Cf. Yaḥya ibn Ādam, *Kitāb al-Kharāj*, p. 167 (art. 610).

[7] This paragraph seems to have been borrowed, with very slight changes, from al-Māwardi, *al-Aḥkām as-Sulṭānīyah*, pp. 264-265.

[8] Cf. Muḥammad ibn al-Ḥasan, *al-Jāmiʿ aṣ-Ṣaghīr*, p. 22, and al-Māwardi, *al-Aḥkām as-Sulṭānīyah*, p. 264.

[9] Aṭ-Ṭabari, *Ikhtilāf*, p. 226_{9-10}; al-Māwardi, *al-Aḥkām as-Sulṭānīyah*, p. 263.

[10] Muḥammad ibn ʿAbd ar-Raḥmān. Jurist of al-Madīnah, A.H. 80 - A.H. 159. See an-Nawawi, *Tahdhīb al-Asmāʾ*, pp. 111-112.

[11] ʿAbd ar-Raḥmān ibn ʿAmr, A.H. 88/A.D. 707 - A.H. 157/A.D. 774. Founder of a school of jurisprudence that disappeared at an early date. See article "al-Awzāʿī" by A. J. Wensinck in *E.I.*

[12] Cf. Muḥammad ibn al-Ḥasan, *al-Jāmiʿ aṣ-Ṣaghīr*, p. 22, and aṭ-Ṭabari, *Ikhtilāf*, p. 223_{10-14}.

[13] A slave who enters into a contractual arrangement with his master, in accordance with which he buys his freedom. See article "ʿAbd" by Th. W. Juynboll in *E.I.*

[14] Cf. Yaḥya ibn Ādam, *Kitāb al-Kharāj*, pp. 168-169 (art. 617); aṭ-Ṭabari, *Ikhtilāf*, p. 223_{18-20}.

Abu Yūsuf has said that if a waste land located within a territory conquered by force is brought under cultivation by a Muslim, it becomes his property.[1] If this land is fed by *kharāj* water, it is regarded as *kharāj* land. But if he contrives a well therefor, or relies upon the water of the heavens for its irrigation,[2] it is regarded as tithe land. Bishr has said that it is tithe land whether it is irrigated by *kharāj* water or not.

Abu Yūsuf has stated that if a country happens to have an ancient foreign custom that Islam has neither changed nor voided, and if some people complain of it to the *imām* and request him to remove its vexations, he may not do so. But Mālik and ash-Shāfiʿi have maintained that he may do so, even though this custom be ancient. For it is incumbent upon him to remove every unjust custom instituted by a Muslim, to say nothing of those instituted by the people of unbelief.

This much suffices on the rules governing *kharāj* land.

Tithe Lands

And now we turn to the legal provisions governing tithe lands, of which there are six kinds.[3]

One kind comprises those lands whose owners embraced Islam while still in occupation and possession thereof, such as the Yaman, al-Madīnah, and aṭ-Ṭā'if. The tax levied upon them is the tithe. Certain jurists have included in this category the lands of those Arabs from whom naught was accepted save Islam or the sword. For there was a difference between those who embraced Islam voluntarily and those who embraced it by compulsion. The Prophet actually demonstrated this difference by granting to the people of aṭ-Ṭā'if, whose adherence to Islam was voluntary, that which he did not grant to others, such as declaring their valley inviolate, leaving the groups within their community undisturbed, and providing that none be given command over them save one from among them.

From the people of Dūmat al-Jandal he took a portion of their property, leaving them in possession of their fortress but divesting them of their *ḥalqah* (war equipment) which consisted of horses and weapons. For they came forth voluntarily, desiring to embrace Islam. After the Muslims had conquered their lands, the Prophet gave them a pledge of security, but fearing their treachery, he took away their weapons. Abu Bakr dealt in a similar manner with the apostates (*ahl ar-riddah*) after their defeat. He imposed upon them a choice between a war of expulsion and an abasing peace, whereby he would divest them of their weapons and mounts.

Another kind is that part of a wasteland (*arḍ al-mawāt*) brought under cultiva-

[1] This legal principle is based upon the following *ḥadīth* of the Prophet: "If a man brings a wasteland under cultivation, it is his." Al-Bukhāri, *Ṣaḥīḥ*, ed. Krehl, II, 71. This is also found in several other *ḥadīth* collections. See *C.T.M.*, I, 539. See also Ibn Sallām, *Kitāb al-Amwāl*, pp. 285-293; Abu Yūsuf, *Kitāb al-Kharāj*, pp. 37-38; and Yaḥya ibn Ādam, *Kitāb al-Kharāj*, pp. 84-90 (art. 266-284).

[2] This legal principle is based upon the *ḥadīth* "one tenth is to be levied on that which is irrigated by the water of the heavens, by springs, and by other natural means, while one half of one tenth is to be levied on that which is irrigated by artificial means." Al-Bukhāri, *Ṣaḥīḥ*, I, 377. This *ḥadīth* is found in most collections. See *C.T.M.*, II, 481. Cf. Yaḥya ibn Ādam, *Kitāb al-Kharāj*, pp. 115-123 (art. 364-395), and Abu Yūsuf, *Kitāb al-Kharāj*, p. 37.

[3] Cf. Ibn Sallām, *Kitāb al-Amwāl*, pp. 512-513 (art. 1559-1564); al-Māwardi, *al-Aḥkām as-Sulṭānīyah*, pp. 254-255, and Abu Yūsuf, *Kitāb al-Kharāj*, p. 39.

tion by the Muslims, to which neither a Muslim nor a *muʿāhad* (covenanter) has a title. The owners become subject to the payment of tithe on the yield thereof.

There is also that land with which the *imāms* enfeoff (*yuqṭiʿu*) certain Muslims. When a Muslim comes into possession of a fief (*iqṭāʿ*), he becomes subject to the payment of *zakāh* thereon, which is also the tithe.

Another kind is that property which accrues to a Muslim from lands conquered by force and distributed by the *imāms* among those Muslims who pressed upon them by horse and camel (*awjafa ʿalayhā*).

Then there is the land that passes into the hands of a Muslim from the *ṣafāyā* [1] (choice spoils) which ʿUmar ibn al-Khaṭṭāb set aside as his share of the lands of the Sawād and which had belonged in particular to Chosroes and to members of his household.

Another kind is that part of his lands which the enemy evacuated and which thus passed into the hands of those Muslims who occupied it and resided therein, such as *thughūr* (frontier fortresses).

Fifths (*Akhmās*)

As regards the fifths, there is the fifth that is levied on the *ghanīmah*, which the Prophet used to take.

Another is the fifth that is levied upon the *maʿdan* [2] (mine). This word derives from "*ʿadana bil-makān*," signifying "to reside and be fixed in a place, becoming an inherent quality thereof," as in the case of gold, silver, iron, and copper, and whatsoever is extracted by skill from the soil of the earth. A fifth is levied thereon.

Another is the yield of the sea (*sayb al-baḥr*), [3] which is what the sea casts up, such as ambergris and the like, as though it were a gift of the sea. A fifth is levied thereon.

Another is that which the tithe collector (*al-ʿāshir*) levies upon property conveyed in commerce by the Muslims, *dhimmis*, and *ḥarbis*.

Next we say, men of learning have declared that whenever the people of a fortress pay ransom in order that they may be left unmolested, and the *imām* considers it advantageous to the religion and to the Muslim community, that [which accrues from the] fortress is for the Muslim community as a whole. Thus if [Muslim] troops march upon a fortress whose defenders posses the power to resist (*fi minʿah*) and against whom they do not prevail by force, the ransom [obtained therefrom] is not regarded as *ghanīmah* for those participating in the siege to the exclusion of the Muslims as a whole. [4] Therefore, everything that is taken from the *ḥarbis* by way of ransom is regarded as public property rather than as the private property of those participating in the siege.

Yaḥya ibn Ādam [5] has said:

> I have heard Sharīk say that *kharāj* land is that land concerning which a

[1] See al-Māwardi, *al-Aḥkām as-Sulṭānīyah*, p. 332; Abu Yūsuf, *Kitāb al-Kharāj*, p. 32; Yaḥya ibn Ādam, *Kitāb al-Kharāj*, p. 45; al-Balādhuri, *Futūḥ al-Buldān*, pp. 32-35; and aṭ-Ṭabari, *Ikhtilāf*, pp. 140-141 (art. 93-94).

[2] Cf. Abu Yūsuf, *Kitāb al-Kharāj*, p. 12.

[3] This principle is traced to the following *ḥadīth* of the Prophet: "One-fifth is levied upon the *suyūb* (sing. *sayb*)." See Ibn al-Athīr, *an-Nihāyah*, p. 198, and Abu Yūsuf, *Kitāb al-Kharāj*, pp. 39-40.

[4] Cf. Ibn Sallām, *Kitāb al-Amwāl*, pp. 252-255.

[5] Jurist, born *circa* A.H. 140; died A.H. 203. See article "Yaḥya ibn Ādam" by J. Schacht in *E.I.*

treaty of peace has been concluded, stipulating the payment of *kharāj* to the Muslims.

Yaḥya has also said:

> I asked Sharīk, 'What, then, is the status of the Sawād?' He answered, 'This territory was taken by force and is therefore *fay'*, but its inhabitants were allowed to remain therein and a certain tax, which they were to pay annually, was levied upon them.' [1] He also said, 'And that part of the Sawād which lies before the mountains is *fay'*, while that part which lies beyond is *ṣulḥ*.' [2]

Abu Ḥanīfah has said that that concerning which a peace treaty is concluded [3] with the Muslims should be regarded as *fay'*. The Prophet is reported to have said:

> You may perchance fight certain people who may ward off your attack with their property rather than with themselves and their children, and conclude with you a treaty of peace. Take not in excess of that, for such is not lawful unto you. [4]

Certain jurists have permitted an increase in the tax rate, in case of surplus, on that property of those conquered by peace treaty which is capable of bearing such an increase. In this matter they have followed the traditions and practices of their predecessors. [5] There is a difference, however, between conquest by peace treaty and conquest by force of arms, although both come under the tithe and the *kharāj*. Hence there has been disagreement concerning the property of those conquered by force of arms, but none concerning the property of those conquered by peace treaty.

Certain learned investigators disapprove of the purchase of the lands of those conquered by force, but there is unanimous agreement that the purchase of the lands of those conquered by peace treaty is permissible. [6] For the latter, having concluded a peace treaty prior to their being overcome and defeated, remain in possession of their lands, retaining the titles thereto.

Ash-Shāfiʿi has said:

> If the people of *ṣulḥ* neglected for a number of years to pay the consideration for which they were granted a peace treaty, by reason of poverty or ignorance, the discharge of that obligation would still be required of them when they prosper. [7]

On the other hand, Abu Ḥanīfah has said:

> They shall be responsible for the payment of that which is due on them from the time of the resumption of payment, but nothing is due on them from the past. [8]

1 This passage closely parallels the text of Yaḥya ibn Ādam, *Kitāb al-Kharāj*, p. 20 (art. 17).

2 Cf. *ibid.*, p. 21 (art. 19).

3 The verb *ṣūliḥa*, occurring in the phrase *ma ṣūliḥa ʿalayhi al-Muslimūn* (that concerning which a peace treaty was concluded with the Muslims), appears incorrectly as *ṣūliḥu* in the German edition.

4 Cf. Ibn Sallām, *Kitāb al-Amwāl*, p. 143, and Yaḥya ibn Ādam, *Kitāb al-Kharāj*, pp. 75-76 (art. 237). The first of these is closer to Yāqūt's version.

5 Cf. Ibn Sallām, *Kitāb al-Amwāl*, pp. 41-42, and al-Māwardi, *al-Aḥkām as-Sulṭānīyah*, pp. 259-261.

6 Yaḥya ibn Ādam, *Kitāb al-Kharāj*, p. 23 (art. 27) and p. 24 (art. 34). See also Ibn Sallām, *Kitāb al-Amwāl*, p. 156 (art. 436-437); al-Māwardi, *al-Aḥkām as-Sulṭānīyah*, pp. 77-86; and aṭ-Ṭabari, *Ikhtilāf*, p. 220_{3-4}

7 Cf. ash-Shāfiʿi, *Kitāb al-Umm*, IV, 122.

8 Cf. al-Māwardi, *al-Aḥkām as-Sulṭānīyah*, p. 252, and aṭ-Ṭabari, *Ikhtilāf*, pp. 211_{5-6} and 223_{17-18}.

This is also the view of Sufyān ath-Thawri.

Mālik and the people of the Ḥijāz have said that if a man of the people of *ṣulḥ* embraces Islam, tithe is levied upon his land and his share is deducted from [the collective tax imposed by] the peace treaty arrangements. Thus if all the people of Cyprus were to embrace Islam, their lands would become tithe lands because they would not have been taken forcibly from them. For they had paid ransom in order to avoid being killed. [1]

Abu Ḥanīfah, Sufyān, and the people of Iraq treat *ṣulḥ* like *fay'*. Thus if the people of *ṣulḥ* were to embrace Islam, they would be treated as they were treated in their former state under *ṣulḥ*. Nothing would be added to their obligations. Moreover, if they have to break their compact, in case *ṣulḥ* revenues are needed for their sustenance, they may do so.

[1] See Ibn Sallām, *Kitāb al-Amwāl,* pp. 171-174 (art. 467-474).

CHAPTER FIVE

ON SOME ACCOUNTS OF COUNTRIES

AL-ḤAJJĀJ [1] [ibn Yūsuf] said to Zādhānfarrūkh, [2] "Tell me of the Arabs and their countries."

"May God prosper the prince, I am a better judge of the Persians than of the Arabs," said Zādhānfarrūkh.

"You shall tell me," al-Ḥajjāj demanded.

"Ask what you will," replied Zādhānfarrūkh.

Then al-Ḥajjāj said, "Tell me of the people of al-Kūfah."

"They settled in the vicinity of the people of the Sawād and partook of their virtues and generosity," answered Zādhānfarrūkh.

"And the people of al-Baṣrah?" al-Ḥajjāj inquired.

"They settled in the vicinity of the Khūz and partook of their deceit and parsimony," said Zādhānfarrūkh.

"And the people of the Ḥijāz?" asked al-Ḥajjāj.

"They settled in the vicinity of the Sūdān [Blacks] and partook of their light-mindedness and merrymaking," Zādhānfarrūkh said.

Al-Ḥajjāj was angry.

Whereupon Zādhānfarrūkh said, "May God exalt you, you are not one of them —a Ḥijāzi. You are a man of the people of Syria."

"Tell me of the people of Syria," commanded al-Ḥajjāj.

"They settled in the vicinity of the Byzantines and partook of their gentleness, courage, and crafts," said Zādhānfarrūkh. [3]

And Muʿāwiyah [4] [ibn Abi Sufyān] asked Ibn al-Kawwā' [5] about the people of al-Kūfah.

Ibn al-Kawwā' said, "Of all people, [they are] the most searching after a minor sin (*ṣaghīrah*) and the least mindful of a major one (*kabīrah*)." [6]

[1] Governor-general of Iraq and the eastern provinces of the Umayyad empire. A.D. 661 - A.D. 714. See article "al-Ḥadjdjādj" by H. Lammens in *E.I.*

[2] Finance Minister of al-Ḥajjāj. The most comprehensive study of his career is found in Sprengling, "From Persian to Arabic," *A.J.S.L.*, LVI (1939), 175-224, 325-336. This name appears as Zadān Farrūkh in both the German and Egyptian editions. The name-form adopted above is in accordance with that given in Ferdinand Justi, *Iranisches Namenbuch*, (Marburg, 1895), p. 377.

[3] The same anecdote is found in Ibn al-Faqīh. The wording of the two versions is almost identical. See *B.G.A.*, V, 114.

[4] The first Umayyad caliph. A.D. 600 or 610 - A.D. 680. See article "Muʿāwiya" by H. Lammens in *E.I.*

[5] ʿAbd Allāh ibn ʿAmr of the Banu Yashkur, a pro-ʿAlid leader prominent during the struggle between ʿAli and Muʿāwiyah. See Wüstenfeld, *Geschichtschreiber*, p. 3.

[6] A major or grave sin, *kabīrah* has been defined as "that which is absolutely forbidden and for which an irrevocable punishment, in this world and in the next, is prescribed by a definite provision." See al-Jurjāni, *Taʿrīfāt*, p. 162, and article "Khaṭī'a" by A. J. Wensinck in *E. I.*

"And the people of al-Baṣrah?" Muʿāwiyah asked.

"[They are] sheep that come forth together but return apart," replied Ibn al-Kawwā'.

"And the people of the Ḥijāz?" Muʿāwiyah inquired.

"Of all people, [they are] the quickest to [rise in] rebellion and the feeblest therein," Ibn al-Kawwā' answered.

"And the people of Egypt?" asked Muʿāwiyah.

"[They are] hard-working, keen-minded, and strong—the devourers of him who prevails," declared Ibn al-Kawwā'.

"And the people of Mosul?" Muʿāwiyah inquired.

"[They are] the necklace of a nation, embellished with a bead of every kind," said Ibn al-Kawwā'.

"And the people of al-Jazīrah?" asked Muʿāwiyah.

"[They are] the sweepings of that which is between the two countries," answered Ibn al-Kawwā'.

Whereupon Muʿāwiyah was silent.

"Ask me further," said Ibn al-Kawwā'.

But Muʿāwiyah was silent.

"You will ask me, or I shall speak to you of that which you avoid," Ibn al-Kawwā' insisted.

"Tell me of the people of Syria," said Muʿāwiyah.

"Of all people, [they are] the most obedient to man and the most disobedient to God," Ibn al-Kawwā' answered. [1]

The ancients divided the kings of the earth into various classes. [2] All kings, they held, acknowledged the greatness of the King of Babylonia. They recognized that he was the first among the kings of the world. Among them he was as the moon among the planets, for his was the noblest of climes and he was the wealthiest of kings, the best natured among them, and the one with the most firmness and tact. [3] Kings subject to him called him Shāhānshāh, [4] which means king of

[1] An identical version of this anecdote appears in Ibn al-Faqīh, *B.G.A.*, V, 135. See also Ibn ʿAbd Rabbihi, *al-ʿIqd al-Farīd*, ed. Aḥmad Amīn, et al. (Cairo, 1949), VI, 250.

[2] This section, up to the end of the poem on page 78, appears in al-Masʿūdi's *Murūj*, I, 357-359. With the exception of one sentence found in al-Masʿūdi but not in Yāqūt (see footnote 3), and a few minor errors by the copyists of the manuscripts, the two versions are almost identical. Yāqūt's indebtedness to al-Masʿūdi is beyond doubt. For this information appears to be substantially the same as that which was contained in the observations made by the Chinese Emperor to an Arab traveler, a descendent of the Qurayshite al-Aswad ibn Habbār. (*Ibid.*, 314-315.) Al-Masʿūdi tells us that this information was imparted to him by Abu Yazīd Muḥammad ibn Yazīd as-Sīrāfi, who met and interviewed the Qurayshite traveler upon his return from China. (*Ibid.*, 321.)

[3] At this point the following sentence, which is missing in Yāqūt's version, is found in al-Masʿūdi: "This used to be true of the kings of this clime, but not at this time which is the year A.H. 322." (*Ibid.*, 357.)

[4] For a thesaurus or concordance of the names, titles and appellations of the Persian kings, especially as found in contemporary documents, see Robert Dick Wilson, "Titles of the Persian Kings," *Festschrift Eduard Sachau*, ed. Gotthold Weil, (Berlin, 1915), pp. 179-207. See also article "Shah" by V. F. Büchner in *E.I.* According to a *ḥadīth* transmitted by Abu Hurayrah, the Prophet is reported to have expressed strong disapproval of this title: "The most abominable of names to God on the Day of Judgment is that of a man who calls himself King of Kings (*Malik al-Amlāk*)." After giving this *ḥadīth*, al-Bukhāri says, on the authority of Sufyān, that the term *Malik al-Amlāk* means *Shāhānshāh*. See al-Bukhāri, *Ṣaḥīḥ*, ed. Krehl, IV, 159-160. It is interesting to note that in *Hazvārish*, the Aramaic term *Malkān-malkā* was read *Shāhānshāh*. See E. G. Brown, *A Literary History of Persia*, (Cambridge, 1929), I, 66, 71, 75.

kings. His position in the world was as the heart in the body, or the centerpiece in a necklace.

Next to him in greatness was the King of India. He was the king of wisdom and the king of victory, [1] for among the great kings, wisdom was from India.

Next in rank to the King of India was the King of China. He was the king of public welfare, statesmanship, and skillfulness in crafts. For none among the kings of the world showed more concern for his subjects, troops, and supporters, or took better care of them, than the King of China. He possessed great strength and power and was invincible, for he had ready troops, equipment, and weapons, and his men possessed abundant rations, like those of the King of Babylonia.

Next to him in rank was [one of] [2] the King[s] of the Turks, the ruler of the city of Kūshān, [3] who is King of the Toghuzghuz. He was called the king of beasts and the king of horses. For among the kings of the world there was none whose men were more hardy than his, nor was there a king more intrepid in the shedding of blood, or possessed of more horses. His kingdom was between the country of China and the deserts of Khurāsān. He was known by the more general name of Irkhān. [4] The Turks had many kings, and comprised various races, possessed of strength and power, who did not submit to any king. However, there was not one among these kings who was comparable to him in power. [5]

Then there was the King of the Byzantines. He was called the king of men, for among the kings of the world there was none whose men were more handsome than his.

After these, kings attained equality.

One of the poets has said: [6]

> Twain is the Mansion: Īwān [7] and Ghumdān; [8]
> Twain the dominion: Sāsān and Qaḥṭān.

[1] The al-Mas'ūdi text has *fiyalah* (elephants) instead of *ghalabah* (victory) as in Yāqūt. Al-Mas'ūdi, *Murūj*, I, 357.

[2] This addition is from al-Mas'ūdi, who has the phrase *malik min mulūk at-Turk* (one of the kings of the Turks) instead of the phrase *malik at-Turk* (the king of the Turks). *Ibid.*, 358.

[3] For a discussion of the Kushan empire, see Minorsky, *Ḥudūd*, pp. 230-232, and J. H. Kramers, "Peshāwar", *Analecta Orientalia*, pp. 368 ff.

[4] Referring specifically to al-Mas'ūdi's use of this term, Minorksy maintains that it should be restored to Uyghur-khān. *Ibid.*, p. 267.

[5] Yudāri, which means "cares for," should be read *yudāni*, which means "approaches" or "comes close to." See al-Mas'ūdi, *Murūj*, I, 358.

[6] This poem is by 'Iṣābah al-Jarjarāy. This poet seems to have been known by another name, for under the entry "Jarjarāya" (*Mu'jam*, II, 55), Yāqūt refers to him as follows: "'Iṣābah al-Jarjarāy whose name is Ibrahīm ibn Badhām who has a collection of poems and about whom there are stories and anecdotes. 'Awn ibn Muḥammad al-Kindi transmitted from him." Yāqūt has twice quoted the above verse, both times as part of a larger quotation. It is interesting to note that the two versions differ, for in both instances Yāqūt seems to have faithfully copied the poem as he found it in the source he used. Here the poem appears as part of a larger unacknowledged quotation from al-Mas'ūdi (see footnote 2, p. 76), while in *Mu'jam*, II, 412-413, it appears as part of another unacknowledged passage from Ibn al-Faqīh, *B.G.A.*, V, 316. In addition to differences in the wording of the two versions, it will be noted that the above version comprises six lines of verse, whereas the other version comprises only four. For an English rendition of this poem, see al-Mas'ūdi, *Meadows of Gold and Mines of Precious Stones*, ed. and trans. Aloys Sprenger, (London, 1849), I, 369. For a French version, see al-Mas'ūdi, *Murūj*, I, 359.

[7] Known also as Ṭāq Kisra (Chosroes' Arch), a vast rectangular hall enclosed by walls on three sides and open on the fourth. The magnificent ruin of the Īwān, with its immense unsupported arch, is all that remains of the palace which stood in the Sasanid capital of al-Madā'in. The latter is now a village about 40 miles south of Baghdad known as Salmān Pāk after the name of the Companion, Salmān al-Fārisi, who is buried there. See articles "Aiwān"

The land is Fārs, the clime is Babylon,
Islām is Mecca, the world Khurāsān.

The desert twain, which fairness have attained,
Bukhāra and the Shah's Balkh are Tūrān.

Baylaqān, Ṭabaristān, and that which surrounds them,
The Lakz and their Shirwān, the Jīl and their Jīlān. [1]

In his rank has been placed every man,
Marzubān, [2] Patrician, [3] and Ṭarkhān; [4]

Thus Chosroes among Persians, and Caesar among the Rūm,
The Negus among Ethiopes, among the Turks Khāqān. [5]

It has been related that ʿUmar ibn al-Khaṭṭāb asked Kaʿb al-Aḥbār [6] about the country and the conditions thereof. Kaʿb al-Aḥbār said:

Oh commander of the faithful, when God, may He be praised and exalted, created things, He attached something to everything.

Thus reason said, 'I am going to Iraq,' and learning said, 'I am with you.'

Wealth said, 'I am going to Syria,' and rebellion said, 'I am with you.'

Poverty said, 'I am going to the Ḥijāz,' and contentment said, 'I am with you.'

Cruelty said, 'I am going to the Maghrib,' and bad manners said, 'I am with you.'

Beauty said, 'I am going to the East,' and good manners said, 'I am with you.'

Misery said, 'I am going to the desert,' and health said, 'I am with you.'

and "Kisrā" by Cl. Huart in *E.I.* See also Honigmann, "Ktesiphon" in Pauly-Wissowa, *Real-Encyclopädie*, Supplementband IV, 1102-1119.

[8] An ancient castle near Ṣanʿāʾ, the capital of the Yaman, celebrated for its size and splendor, now in ruins. See article "Ghumdān" by Fr. Buhl in *E.I.*

[1] Linking the Lakz with the Shirwān in the above verse is probably based upon the connection that existed between them after the annexation of the Lakz territory by the King of Shirwān, Muḥammad ibn Yazīd. Minorsky cites al-Masʿūdi, *Murūj*, II, 5, to the effect that the Lakz kingdom was the bulwark of the Shirwān kingdom. See Minorsky, *Ḥudūd*, p. 455.

[2] The Arabic form of the Pahlavi *Marzpān*. The title of the provincial governors in the Sasanian Empire, especially of the markgraves or "wardens of the marches." See article "Marzubān" by J. H. Kramers in *E. I.*

[3] According to al-Khwārizmi, *al-Biṭrīq* (Patrician) is a Byzantine general in charge of 10,000 men. See al-Khwārizmi, *Mafātīḥ al-ʿUlūm*, p. 128.

[4] Al-Khwārizmi describes *aṭ-Ṭarkhān* as a Turkish nobleman (*ibid.*, p. 120), and as a Byzantine general in charge of 5,000 men and subordinate to the *Biṭrīq* (*ibid.*, 129). According to A.Z. Validi Togan, *Ibn Fadlan's Reisebericht*, p. 30. note 3, this is a Turkish title current among the Khazars. Minorsky, however, thinks that *Tarkhan* is an Arabic reproduction of the Greek title *Turmarch*. See V. Minorsky, "Marvazi on the Byzantines," *Mélange Henri Grégoire*: *Annuaire de l'Institut de Philologie et d'Histoire Orientales et Slaves*, (1950) X, 455-469.

[5] The Arabic transcription of the Turkish royal title *Qāghān*. According to al-Khwārizmi, this title means Grand King of the Turks. For *khān*, he says, means chief, and *Khāqān* is the *Khān* of *Khāns*, which is like the Persian usage of Shāhānshāh. (*Mafātīḥ al-ʿUlūm*, p. 120). See also article "*Khāḳān*" by W. Barthold in *E.I.*

[6] Abu Isḥāq Kaʿb ibn Mātiʿ, Yamani Jewish convert to Islam and oldest authority on Jewish Muslim traditions among the Arabs. See article "Kaʿb al-Aḥbār" by M. Schmitz in *E.I.*

Here end the words of Kaʿb al-Aḥbār.[1]

And God is the guide to what is right. To Him we revert, and to Him is our ultimate return.[2]

[1] This version is almost identical with that found in al-Masʿūdi, *Murūj*, III, 130-131. The same story also appears in an-Nuwayri, *Nihāyat al-Arab*, I, 292; at-Taghribirdi, *an-Nujūm az-Zāhirah fi Mulūk Miṣr w-al-Qāhirah*, (Cairo, 1929), I, 51; and al-Maqrīzi, *Khiṭaṭ*, I, 50. Like the majority of medieval Muslim works on history and geography, all of the above-mentioned books include sections dealing with the merits and demerits of cities and countries, and the characteristics of their inhabitants. The origin of this practice may be traced to the sayings of the Prophet, some of which are genuine *ḥadīths* and some merely attributed to him.

[2] It is perhaps fitting at this point to examine the two quotations from al-Masʿūdi's *Murūj*, occurring in this chapter, in the light of the findings of Justus Heer. According to this writer (Heer, *Die historischen und geographischen Quellen in Jāqūt's geographischem Wörterbuch*, p. 13), al-Masʿūdi's name is mentioned only ten times in the *Muʿjam*, each mention being in connection with a citation. All ten citations are from Vols. I, II, and III of the Barbier de Meynard and Pavet de Courteille edition of the *Murūj*. This fact has led Heer to suggest the possibility that Yāqūt may have had access to only the first three volumes of the *Murūj*. With regard to the textual variations which exist between Yāqūt's version of these citations and al-Masʿūdi's version as it stands in the *Murūj*, Heer suggests the possibility that the author of the *Muʿjam* may have used another source, such as the augmented edition of the *Murūj* often referred to in the *Tanbīh*. Now to come to the two quotations found in this chapter. Unlike the ten citations referred to above, both of these quotations are faithful reproductions from al-Masʿūdi's text of the *Murūj*. Also, unlike the citations in question, these quotations are unacknowledged. This fact raises the question as to how many such unacknowledged quotations there are in the *Muʿjam*. It is interesting to note that the first quotation, which occurs on pp. 76-78 above, is from Vol. I of the *Murūj* (see footnote 2, p. 76), while the second quotation, which occurs on pp. 78-79, is from Vol. III of that work (see footnote 1 above).

Stockum

8.VIII.69